TORAH
FOR THE
NATIONS

DANIEL M. DICKENS

First Printing, 2017

ISBN: 978-1545573945

ABOUT THE AUTHOR

DANIEL DICKENS grew up as a Baptist Christian in the lower peninsula of Michigan. While in his first year at Liberty University in Lynchburg, VA, Daniel became very serious about his faith and devoted himself to studying the Christian Bible and knowing the Creator.

After praying and reading the Bible for an hour at sunrise each morning for one year, Daniel felt as if G-d wanted him to live homeless for three weeks until his college classes resumed at the end of the summer. A friend dropped him off under a bridge in Lynchburg, VA with only a blanket, Bible, and journal in a backpack.

Daniel opened up to Genesis 1:1 and began reading and journaling. Three weeks later he was convinced that the Torah was not done away with. A few months later, Daniel married and began having children.

While attaining his degree in Biblical Studies at the largest evangelical university in the world, he was presented with many challenges. Nevertheless, he continued to teach that the Torah was valid as he helped the poor, pastored, and planted churches.

After a series of events, Daniel found himself pastoring in a church that grew out of home meetings. Eventually the other leadership couldn't stand hearing Daniel teach about Sabbaths, feasts, and the Torah, even though the church members were practically begging for more Torah. Finally, it culminated in a meeting that ended the church, and all remaining funds were given to charity.

Daniel was greatly disappointed by all of this and began searching around for groups that believed in the Christian Bible and the Torah. After several strange and disappointing experiences, he found a very kind and loving Messianic/Hebrew Roots group that met in the county. He became an integral part of that group for years as he continued to learn more and more Torah.

Gradually, Daniel found it increasingly more difficult to participate in Messianic groups because the learning was not kosher. Those that attempted to communicate kosher Torah learning were hushed, and even told by leadership, "We believe in Yeshua, and if you learn from Mishnah and Talmud, maybe this isn't the place for you."

Daniel had similar experience at the other Messianic/Hebrew Roots groups he visited over the years. Eventually he realized that Messianic/Hebrew Roots groups are actually another sect of Christianity attempting to force the perfect peg of Torah into a deep rooted cross-shaped hole of Christian theology about a man-god.

Through a long process over years of learning and growing, Daniel now identifies as a simple Noahide that desires to know HaShem through the light of the Torah as preserved and taught by Orthodox Judaism.

Daniel's desire is to help others on a similar journey to know HaShem, live a righteous life, and have peace in this world through the knowledge of Torah.

TABLE OF CONTENTS

PREFACE 4
THE ONE TRUE G-D 7
  This is our G-d. 9
  Not with you alone! 12
TORAH 17
  Moses writes about his death. 19
ORAL TORAH 23
  Hillel & Shammai: Two Laws 26
SANHEDRIN 31
  Hillel & Shammai: On One Foot 34
MISHNAH 37
  Rabbi Yehudah: Body & Soul 39
GEMARAH & TALMUD 43
  Moshe Rabbeinu & Rabbi Akiva 44
POST-TALMUDIC SCHOLARSHIP 49
  Rashi 49
  Rambam 50
  Rabbi Yoseph Karo 52
  Romm Publishing House 53
INTERPRETATION 57
  Rabbi Yonatan: Following the Majority 60
TORAH FOR THE NATIONS 65
  Are non-Jews required to keep Torah? 67
  The Covenant with Noah 67
  What is a Bnei Noach or Noahide? 68
  Can I do *mitzvot*? 69
  Shemayah & Avtalion: Converts Teaching Hillel 70
NOAHIDE LAWS 75
  1) The prohibition against worship of false gods. 77
  2) The prohibition against cursing G-d 81
  3) The prohibition against murder. 82
  4) The prohibition against incest and adultery. 83
  5) The prohibition against theft. 84

6) The command to establish laws and courts of justice. 85
7) The prohibition against eating flesh with its lifeblood. 85
IDOLATRY 91
False g-ds. 93
Idol worship. 95
Dealings with idolaters. 100
False evangelists & false prophets. 101
Hillel & The Floating Skull 105
MASHIACH 109
What is a *Mashiach*? 111
How will we know who the *Mashiach* is? 112
What is the *Messianic Era*? 114
Is *Mashiach* G-d? 117
Can *Mashiach* die for sins? 119
Is *Mashiach* the Passover lamb? 122
When will *Mashiach* come? 123
TESHUVAH 129
Confession & Atonement 129
Complete Teshuvah 132
Divine Reward & Retribution 135
Free Will 138
Drawing Near 139
Olam Habah (The World to Come) 142
Rabbi Saadia Gaon: If I had known about G-d 145
WHERE DO I START? 153
Love HaShem! 153
Rabbi Shimon: For the Sake of the Mitzvah 155
Learn from kosher sources 158
Chumash 158
Tenakh 159
The Seven 159
Learning Hebrew 160
Should I go to a synagogue? 160
Conversion 161
What will my friends and family think? 161
INDEX 164

PREFACE

Thus said the L-rd of Hosts: Peoples and the inhabitants of many cities shall yet come—the inhabitants of one shall go to the other and say, "Let us go and entreat the favor of HaShem, let us seek the L-rd of Hosts; I will go, too." The many peoples and the multitude of nations shall come to seek the L-rd of Hosts in Jerusalem and to entreat the favor of HaShem.

Thus said the L-rd of Hosts: In those days, ten men from nations of every tongue will take hold—they will take hold of every Jew by a corner of his cloak and say, "Let us go with you, for we have heard that G-d is with you."

Zechariah 8:20-23

More than any other time in history, the people of the nations are grasping for the truth of the Torah. This book is intended for those who want to understand how to connect with the G-d of Israel in the acceptable manner congruent with Orthodox Judaism.

It's commonly accepted by Christianity, Islam, and other religions that the Jewish Bible is a holy book written by true prophets of G-d. However, there are vast differences in the way that Judaism approaches its own texts.

What does Judaism teach about the *Torah, Mishnah,* and *Talmud?* Where did they come from? How do we know the correct interpretation of the Torah? Do Jews add to and take away from the commandments? Are non-Jews second class citizens? What is idolatry? What is a mashiach? How are sins forgiven?

To answer these questions and more, we will travel through the history of Judaism's system of guarding, teaching, and implementing the Torah. It is only after that foundation is laid that we can even begin to understand how ten people from the nations can grasp the corner of every Jew's garment and go with him.

What does HaShem require of me as a non-Jew? The latter portion of this book is devoted to opening up fundamental Orthodox Jewish texts to reveal how non-Jews are to approach the G-d of Abraham, Isaac, and Jacob and live a righteous life in this world (and you may even discover your place in the world to come).

Please do not confuse this content with an apologetic work for Judaism. The goal of this book is to have one organized place for the information someone needs to get plugged into and jump-started in kosher Torah learning.

This book is written for the seeking soul who truly wants to draw near to G-d. I empathize deeply with those who will say, "If only someone had given me this book many years ago!"

I truly hope that you appreciate this book and that it helps you on your journey to know G-d and pursue peace.

THE ONE
TRUE G-D

𝕴 IT IS APPROPRIATE to begin with a little history, which has
been summarized from Rambam's *Mishnah Torah, Hilchos
Avodat Kochavim 1.*

Enosh, along with the wise men of that generation gave
thoughtless council and erred. They honored the stars and spheres
because they said G-d made them and they controlled the world, so
they began serving them.

They made temples to the stars and sacrificed to them, praised
and glorified them, prostrated themselves before them. They wouldn't
say there is no other god except for this star. All of the nations knew

that there is one true G-d, but their foolish error consisted of
conceiving of this emptiness as G-d's will.

> *Who will not fear You, King of the nations, for to You it is fitting.*
> *Among all the wise men of the nations and in all their kingdoms, there is*
> *none like You. They have one foolish and senseless [notion. They conceive*
> *of their] empty teachings as wood.*
>
> *Jeremiah 10:7-8*

Many years passed and false prophets told the nations that G-d
commanded them to serve a star (or all stars), sacrifice to it, offer
libations to it, build a temple, and make an image of it so everyone
could bow to it. The people made images in temples, under trees, and
on tops of mountains and hills.

False prophets continued to proclaim they had prophetic visions
and commanded the nations "Do this," or "Do not do that," and these
practices spread throughout the world, some more distorted than
others. G-d's glorious and awesome name was forgotten by everyone,
and they only worshipped the stars and spheres, except for a few such
as Chanoch, Metushelach, Noach, Shem, and Ever.

Then Abraham was born. Even as a child Abraham thought day
and night, wondering, "How is it possible for the sphere to continue to
revolve without having anyone controlling it? Who is causing it to
revolve?" while he worshipped idols with his father, mother, and all the
people around him.

Eventually he comprehended the way of truth and the path of
righteousness. At 40 years old, Abraham realized there was one G-d
who controlled the sphere, G-d created everything, and there is no
other G-d among all the other entities.

He began telling the people in Ur of the one true G-d and their wrong path they followed. He formulated replies to them and even broke their idols. His arguments were so strong that he overcame them and the king desired to kill him.

After leaving for Charan, he began calling in a loud voice to all people to serve G-d alone. Thousands and myriads gathered around him, and they are called the house of Abraham. He composed texts, taught Isaac and Jacob, and appointed Jacob as a teacher.

Jacob continued to teach all of his children and selected Levi as the leader and established him as head of the academy to teach the way of G-d and observe the *mitzvot* of Abraham. Jacob commanded that the leadership over teaching never depart from Levi's descendants.

The teachings of the one true G-d gathered strength among Jacob's descendants and all who collected around them until there became a nation which knew G-d. The nation learned from the Egyptians when they extended their stay in Egypt, and they all reverted back to star worship, except the tribe of Levi. The tribe of Levi never served false gods.

G-d upheld the oath He made with Abraham and brought forth Moses, our teacher, the master of all prophets. G-d chose Israel as His inheritance, crowned them with *mitzvot* and told them of the path to serve Him, teaching them the judgement prescribed for an idol worshiper and all those who stray after it.

This is our G-d.

How do we know that the G-d of Israel is the one true G-d and there is no other?

Unlike other religions, the validity of Judaism does not rely on miracles, angels, or the revelation of prophets as the proof that HaShem is the one true G-d.

Rather, Judaism is the only religion that claims a national revelation of G-d, instead of an individual revelation, when millions of Jews stood at Mt. Sinai and heard G-d speak.

HaShem said to Moses, "Behold! I come to you in the thickness of the cloud, so that the people will hear as I speak to you, and they will also believe in you forever." (Exodus 19:9)

Furthermore, it is reiterated many times over in the Jewish Scriptures that the nation of Israel should not forget what they all saw and heard together at Mt. Sinai.

[Moses told the Israelites]: 'Only beware for yourself and greatly beware for your soul, lest you forget the things that your eyes have beheld. Do not remove this memory from your heart all the days of your life. Teach your children and your children's children about the day that you stood before HaShem your G-d at Horev [Mount Sinai]...

G-d spoke to you from the midst of the fire, you were hearing the sound of words, but you were not seeing a form, only a sound. He told you of His covenant, instructing you to keep the Ten Commandments, and He inscribed them on two stone tablets.' (Deut.4:9-13)

Ask now of the days that are past, which were before you, since the day that G-d created man on the earth, and ask from one end of heaven to the other, whether such a great thing as this has ever happened or was ever heard of. Did any people ever hear the voice of a god speaking out of the midst of the fire, as you have heard, and still live? Or has any god ever attempted to go and take a nation for himself from the midst of another nation, by trials, by signs, by wonders, and by war, by a mighty hand and an outstretched arm, and by great deeds of terror, all of which HaShem your G-d did for you in Egypt before your eyes? To you it was shown, that you might know that HaShem is G-d; there is no other besides him. Out of heaven he let you hear his voice, that he might discipline you. And on earth he let you see his great fire, and you heard his words out of the midst of the fire.

And because he loved your fathers and chose their offspring after them and brought you out of Egypt with his own presence, by his great power, driving out before you nations greater and mightier than you, to bring you in, to give you their land for an inheritance, as it is this day,

Know therefore today, and lay it to your heart, that HaShem is G-d in heaven above and on the earth beneath; there is no other. Therefore you shall keep his statutes and his commandments, which I command you today, that it may go well with you and with your children after you, and that you may prolong your days in the land that HaShem your G-d is giving you for all time." (Deut. 4:32-40)

Moses called all of Israel and said to them: 'Hear, O Israel, the decrees and the ordinances that I speak in your ears today — learn them, and be careful to perform them. HaShem your G-d sealed a covenant with us at Horev [Mount Sinai]. Not with our forefathers did G-d seal this covenant, but with us — we who are here, all of us alive today. Face to face did G-d speak with you on the mountain from amid the fire.' (Deut. 5:1-4)

Israel was commanded to not only remember what the millions saw and heard, but Israel was also instructed to teach it to their children, and their children's children.

Imagine if you were told right now, "Remember five minutes ago when there was a giant earthquake and G-d spoke to you out of a pillar of fire in a loud booming voice that millions of people all heard and saw at the same time?"

You would immediately know it never happened because you were there and didn't witness such a fantastic event. Nobody would follow such a person that made this claim because it is so easy to prove such a claim false.

On the other hand, if you really did witness such an amazing event along with millions of others that witnessed the same thing at the same time in the same place, you would most certainly take heed to remember it, and it would be impossible to convince that whole nation of millions that they didn't witness such an event if it really did happen.

This is how the revelation of G-d and the Torah was given to Israel. No other religion has ever made such a claim or had the millions of witnesses to testify to it.

This is not to diminish or undermine the great and wondrous works HaShem has done! There were great and amazing miracles performed by Moses our teacher that the magnitude of which has never been repeated by anyone ever. Angels have visited our prophets. HaShem has defeated great and terrible foes and wiped them from the face of the earth.

All of this is true, but we know HaShem is the one true G-d and no other because of the national revelation of Israel at Mt. Sinai.

Not with you alone!

On the last day of Moses' life we see a very intriguing verse, *"Not with you alone do I seal this covenant and oath. I am making it both with those here today before the HaShem our G-d, and also with those not here today."* (Deut. 29:13)

What does it mean, "Not with you alone," and "with those not here today?" The Talmud (Shavuot 39a) explains that this is in reference to all of the souls of future converts that were there at Mount Sinai.

What's even more interesting is that if we take the last letter from each word in the phrase, "both with those here" we have the name of the first convert after the exodus from Egypt, Yitro (יִתְרוֹ). Even though Israel was the only one to accept the Torah as a nation, there are individuals among the nations whose souls sought to accept the 613 commandments at Mount Sinai, but were prevented from realizing their aspirations by the refusal of their peers.

This is why it is required in Jewish Law that the convert to be treated as if he has always been Jewish, never reminding him that he is a convert or treating him differently than any other Jew. It is also forbidden to oppress any foreigner dwelling among Israel, because over and over again HaShem says to remember "you were once slaves in Egypt."

TRUE or FALSE?

1. The men such as Enosh erred in honoring stars and spheres believing they were G-d.

2. Later on, false prophets began worshipping stars as gods and G-d's name was forgotten by everyone.

3. Men such as Chanoch, Metushelach, Noah, Shem, and Ever were not worshippers of the false gods.

4. Abraham worshipped false gods until he was 40 years old.

5. Abraham overcame the people with his arguments to serve G-d alone.

6. Those who gathered around Abraham were called the house of Abraham.

7. Abraham passed the teaching of the one true G-d to Isaac and Jacob.

8. The leadership of teaching has departed from the tribe of Levi because they worshipped false gods.

9. Moses, our teacher, is the master of all prophets.

10. G-d entrusted Israel with the knowledge of what is considered idol worship.

11. Miracles, angles, and revelations of prophets are the primary proof of Judaism's validity.

12. The entire nation of Israel heard G-d speak at Mt. Sinai.

13. G-d came to the people in the thickness of the cloud so they would believe in Moses forever.

14. Every Jew is obligated to teach their children and their children's children what they witnessed at Mt. Sinai.

15. Other religions have a national revelation of G-d.

16. HaShem is the one true G-d and no other.

ANSWERS

1. FALSE

2. TRUE

3. TRUE

4. TRUE

5. TRUE

6. TRUE

7. TRUE

8. FALSE

9. TRUE

10. TRUE

11. FALSE

12. TRUE

13. TRUE

14. TRUE

15. FALSE

16. TRUE

TORAH

THE JEWISH BIBLE IS CALLED the *Tenakh,* which is an acronym for *Torah* (Law), *Nevi'im* (Prophets), and *Khethuvim* (Writings). *Te-Na-Kh.* The *Tenakh* is written in the Hebrew language composed by Hebrew letters called the *Aleph-Beit.*

The Torah is the first five books of the *Tenakh,* also referred to as the Five Books of Moses because it was entirely written down by Moses as he received it word for word from HaShem at Mt. Sinai.

Each book of the Torah is called a *sefer.* The five books of Moses are *Bereishit* (Genesis), *Shemot* (Exodus), *Vayikra* (Leviticus), *Bamidbar* (Numbers), and *Devarim* (Deuteronomy).

The Torah is divided into weekly readings called the *parashat hashavua,* which means "Portion of the Week," but for short we just say *parashah*. The *parashah* corresponding with the current week is read in every Synagogue on Shabbat.

Each *parasha* is divided into seven smaller readings, and we call each one an *aliyah*, which means "elevate" or "go up." It's called an *aliyah* because each Jew that reads an *aliyah* from the Torah "goes up" to the front of the synagogue to read from the Torah. Also, a Jew that moves to Israel is said to have made *aliyah*, because he "went up" or "elevated" to the holy land of Israel.

Each *parashah* has a corresponding *haftorah* reading from the *Nevi'im* (Prophets). Due to the size of the text, the whole Tenakh is not read in the Shabbat services throughout the year. This is not to diminish the rest of the Prophets or their writings (May it never be!), but for practical liturgical reasons pertaining to the weekly Shabbat service.

The Torah tells the history from Creation through end of Moses' life just before Israel crosses over the Jordan River. Also, the Torah contains the eternal Laws that HaShem gave to the Jews at Mt. Sinai that not one letter can ever be added to, subtracted from, or modified. But the Torah is more than history and laws; it's the very tool HaShem used, is using, and will continue to use to create and sustain everything in the entire universe.

The Torah begins with the Hebrew word *bereishit*, which is why the first book of the Torah is called *Bereishit*. *Bereishit 1:1* says, "In the beginning (*bereishit*) G-d created the heavens and the earth." But the word *bereishit* is actually a derivative of another word. This word *bereishit* is the word *reishit* with the prefix of the letter *beit*; *B'Reishit*. *Reishit* is used throughout the Torah in reference to two things; the

Jews, and the Torah. Since the prefix *beit* means "with," we have to ask, "With *what reishit* did G-d create the heavens and the earth?"

Did he create the heavens and the earth with the Jews? At a basic level this doesn't make much sense since the Jewish nation came about much later. So the first verse of the Bible can be interpreted this way, "With *the Torah* G-d created the heavens and the earth."

Pretty cool, huh?

We've already seen three ways the word *Torah* can be used, and we're just getting started. Torah can mean the Five Books of Moses, HaShem's Laws, and it's also the tool by which the universe is created and sustained. We say "is created" and not "was created" because HaShem isn't done creating and sustaining the universe. Not only that, but He gave us His Torah so we can work with him.

Everything HaShem made is important to him. When He created you, he saw that the universe could not go on without you.

Moses writes about his death.

How is it that Moses wrote the words, "And Moses died?" Some erroneously claim that Joshua completed that last part of the Torah, but this is not true. How do we know?

"Take this Torah scroll and put it in the side of the ark of the covenant of HaShem your G-d" (Deut. 31:26). The scroll had already been completed, every letter. HaShem had dictated the entire Torah to Moses at Mt. Sinai, everything past, present, and future that was to be written.

Moses wrote about his own death in tears.

TRUE or FALSE

1. The *Tenakh* is the Jewish Bible.

2. *Tenakh* is an acronym for *Torah, Nevi'im, Khethuvim.*

3. The Hebrew alphabet is called the Aleph-Boot.

4. The first five books of the Jewish Bible are called the *Zohar.*

5. A "book" in Hebrew is "*Sefardic.*"

6. The Five Books of Moses are *Bereishit, Shemot, Vayikra, Bamidbar,* and *Devarim.*

7. A *parashah* is a weekly portion of the Torah.

8. An *aliyah* is a daily portion of the Torah.

9. More laws were added by G-d after Moses died.

10. HaShem used the Torah to create the universe.

ANSWERS

1. TRUE
2. TRUE
3. FALSE
4. FALSE
5. FALSE
6. TRUE
7. TRUE
8. TRUE
9. FALSE
10. TRUE

ORAL TORAH

ASHEM SPOKE THE TORAH to Moses at Mt. Sinai. The small part of the Torah that was written down is the Five books of Moses. The part that remained spoken and was not written down is called the *Torah Shebaal Peh* (Oral Torah). Rambam begins with the following statements in the introduction to Mishnah Torah:

> The mitzvot given to Moses at Mount Sinai were all given together with their explanations, as implied by [Exodus 24:12]: "And I will give you the tablets of stone, the Torah, and the mitzvah."
>
> "The Torah" refers to the Written Law; "the mitzvah," to its explanation. [G-d] commanded us to fulfill "the Torah" according to [the instructions of] "the mitzvah." "The mitzvah" is called the Oral Law.
>
> Moses, our teacher, personally transcribed the entire Torah before he died. He gave a Torah scroll to each tribe and placed another scroll in the

ark as a testimonial, as [Deuteronomy 31:26] states: "Take this Torah scroll and place it [beside the ark...] and it will be there as a testimonial."
"The mitzvah" - i.e., the explanation of the Torah - he did not transcribe. Instead, he commanded it [verbally] to the elders, to Joshua, and to the totality of Israel, as [Deuteronomy 13:1] states: "Be careful to observe everything that I prescribe to you." For this reason, it is called the Oral Law.

Moses taught the *Torah Shebaal Peh* (Oral Torah) to Joshua. Joshua passed it on to the elders of Israel called the *Zekenim*. The *Zekenim* relayed it to the *Nevi'im* (Prophets). The *Nevi'im* continued to teach the *Torah Shebaal Peh* to Israel until the end of the Babylonian captivity and passed it to Ezra's court which was called the *Anshei K'nesset Hagedolah* (Men of the Great Assembly.)

Here's a little time reference to put things into perspective. Moshe received the Torah at Mt. Sinai in 1312 BCE. The *Anshei K'nesset Hagedolah* convened from 410-310BCE. The last Sanhedrin that sat under Rav Ashi during the *diaspora* (dispersion) ended in 358CE. Therefore, the 40 generations of the transmission of *Torah Shebaal Peh* from Moshe until the end of the Sanhedrin led by Rav Ashi was 1,756 years.

These are the forty generations of men that the *Torah Shebaal Peh* was passed down to from Moshe to Rav Ashi.

(Mishnah Torah, Introduction)

1) *Rav Ashi [received the tradition] from Ravva.*
2) *Ravva from Rabbah.*
3) *Rabbah from Rav Huna.*
4) *Rav Huna from Rabbi Yochanan, Rav, and Shemuel.*
5) *Rabbi Yochanan, Rav, and Shemuel from Rabbenu Hakadosh.*
6) *Rabbenu Hakadosh from Rabbi Shimon, his father.*
7) *Rabbi Shimon from Rabban Gamliel, his father.*
8) *Rabban Gamliel from Rabban Shimon, his father.*

9) Rabban Shimon from Rabban Gamliel, the elder, his father.

10) Rabban Gamliel, the elder, from Rabban Shimon, his father.

11) Rabban Shimon from Hillel, his father, and Shammai.

12) Hillel and Shammai from Shemayah and Avtalion.

13) Shemayah and Avtalion from Yehudah and Shimon [ben Shatach].

14) Yehudah and Shimon from Yehoshua ben Perachiah and Nittai of Arbel.

15) Yehoshua and Nittai from Yosse ben Yo'ezer and Yosef ben Yochanan.

16) Yosse ben Yo'ezer and Yosef ben Yochanan from Antignos.

17) Antignos from Shimon the Just.

18) Shimon the Just from Ezra.

Remember, it was at this time of Ezra that the *Anshei K'nesset Hagedolah* was established, and all of the names listed up to this point were the leaders of this Jewish court system established at this point in time.

19) Ezra from Baruch.

20) Baruch from Jeremiah.

21) Jeremiah from Tzefaniah.

22) Tzefaniah from Chabbakuk.

23) Chabbakuk from Nachum.

24) Nachum from Yoel.

25) Yoel from Michah.

26) Michah from Isaiah.

27) Isaiah from Amos.

28) Amos from Hoshea.

29) Hoshea from Zechariah.

30) Zechariah from Yehoyada.

31) Yehoyada from Elisha.

32) Elisha from Elijah.

33) Elijah from Achiah.

34) Achiah from David.

35) David from Shemuel.

36) Shemuel from Eli.

37) Eli from Pinchas.

38) Pinchas from Joshua.

39) Joshua from Moses, our teacher.

40) Moses, our teacher, from the Almighty.

   Thus, [the source of] all these people's knowledge is G-d, the L-rd of Israel.

   All the sages who were mentioned were the leaders of the generations. Among them were heads of academies, heads of the exile, and members of the great Sanhedrin. Together with them in each generation, there were thousands and myriads that heard their [teachings].

Hillel & Shammai: Two Laws

A non-Jewish man once came before Shammai (#12 in the list of forty heads of the Sanhedrin). The man asked Shammai, "How many laws do you have?" Shammai answered, "Two laws: the written and the oral law."

"I believe you in regards to the written law, but I do not believe you as to the oral law. I will convert to Judaism if you teach me the written law," said the man. Shammai rebuked him and sent him away.

The man then went to Hillel (who also sat with Shammai at #12 on the list of forty). Hillel accepted him and began teaching him the alephbet. The next day he began teaching him the same letters backwards.

"You did not teach me so yesterday," objected the man.

Hillel responded, "Yes, yes, my son. Must you not have confidence in what I tell you? You must likewise have confidence in the Oral Law (which appears at first sight different from the written law)."

What does this teach us? The written Torah and Oral Torah are one and the same. At first glance the Oral Torah appears to be different than the Written Torah.

However, if you have confidence in the Oral Torah and learn it, you will see that it is not different than the Written Torah at all. Rather, they complement each other and are inseparable, just as the alephbet, whether recited frontwards or backwards are one and the same.

TRUE or FALSE?

1. All of the *mitzvot* and their explanations were given to Moses at Mt. Sinai.

2. The *mitzvah* is called the *Torah Shebaal Peh*, Oral Law, and the explanation of the Written Law.

3. The *mitzvot* in their entirety were transcribed by Moses.

4. Moses taught the *Torah Shebaal Peh* to Joshua, and Joshua taught the *Zekenim*, and they taught the *Nevi'im* (Prophets).

5. Moses received the Torah at Mt. Sinai in 1312BCE.

6. The *Anshei K'nesset Hagedolah* (Men of the Great Assembly) convened from 410-310BCE.

7. The last Sanhedrin under Rav Ashi sat in 358CE.

8. There were 40 generations of men that the *Torah Shebaal Peh* was passed town to from Moses to Rav Ashi.

9. Ezra was the High Priest while the *Anshei K'nesset Hagedolah* convened.

10. The leaders that received and transmitted the *Torah Shebaal Peh* were not well known and few people heard their teachings.

ANSWERS

1. TRUE
2. TRUE
3. FALSE
4. TRUE
5. TRUE
6. TRUE
7. TRUE
8. TRUE
9. TRUE
10. FALSE

SANHEDRIN

THE GREAT SANHEDRIN is a reference to the *Anshei K'nesset Hagedolah* (Men of the Great Assembly) led by Ezra the High Priest, which convened from 410-310BCE. This spans the time from after the destruction of the First Temple (which was destroyed in 422BCE) and into the early decades of the Second Temple (which was reconstructed from 353-349BCE).

The Great Sanhedrin was the highest court of Isreal, and was made up of the standard 70 members that make up a Sanhedrin. There were 120 men in all that rotated in and out of the *Anshei K'nesset Hagedolah* over the course of a century. Among these leaders were rabbis such as Haggai, Zechariah, Malachi, Mordechai, Daniel, Ezra, and Nehemiah.

The Great Sanhedrin sat during very difficult times and worked diligently with a great weight upon them to enable Israel to survive spiritually during exile. They formalized the prayer services and established synagogues as places of public Torah readings, which is still practiced to this very day.

They prayed fervently for HaShem to remove the inclination toward idolatry from the hearts of people, and HeShem answered their outcry. As a result, prophesy also ceased as atheism replaced idolatry.

The Oral Law was organized into tractates and subjects, which scholars memorized, and was later compiled into a text called the *Mishnah*.

In addition to organizing and formalizing the *mitzvot* into a nationally unified format, the Men of the Great Assembly also put safeguards around the *mitzvot* in accordance with the commandment of the Torah.

> "You shall safeguard My charge not to do any of the customs that are abominable, that were done before you, and not contaminate yourselves through them; I am HaShem your G-d" (Vayikra/Leviticus 18:30).

Rabbinic decree should not be confused with *mitzvot*. The *mitzvot* can't be added to or subtracted from. The Rabbinic decrees were enacted by the Sanhedrin to put a hedge around the *mitzvot* so that nobody would break them and fall into judgment. Rabbinic decrees needed a majority consent, and if any decrees were deemed too difficult to follow, they were revoked.

One of the most notable accomplishments of the Great Sanhedrin is that they established the books of the *Tenakh* as we have them today. As you may have noticed, many of the books in the *Tenakh* were written by or about the leaders of the Great Sanhedrin. They also sealed the *Tenakh* so that no material could be added or subtracted from it.

This also parallels the conclusion of the 1,000 year era of prophesy that came to an end with the last prophet Malachi. This is why no other books other than the *Tenakh* are Scripture or can be elevated to the level of the *Tenakh*.

The *Sanhedrin* is a group of the 70 greatest teachers and judges in Israel. Their Authority is directly from HaShem, passed down directly from Moses, unbroken from generation to generation.

Moses declared the role of the judges in *Shemot*/Exodus 18:16,

> *I judge between a man and between his fellow, and I make know the decrees of G-d and His teachings.*

Moses reiterates the authority of the chain of leaders from Moses in *Devarim*/Deuteronomy 17:11,

> *"According to the teaching that they will teach you and according to the judgment that they will say to you, shall you do; do not deviate from the decision that they will tell you, right or left."*

The Sanhedrin was led by two men called *Zuggot*, which means "pairs." One leader is called the *Nasi*, and it is his duty to oversee the teaching of the Torah to all of the *Sanhedrin* and subsequently all of Israel. The other leader is called the *Av Beit Din*, and he is the head of the court of Law. Ultimately, he makes sure that the judges are ruling rightly according to the Torah.

Even to this day there are Beit Din that oversee different regions all over the world. The last of the five pairs of *Zuggot* were *Nasi* Hillel (the descendant of King David), and the *Av Beit Din* Shammai. The *Zuggot* led for 250 years until the destruction of the 2nd *Beit Hamikdash* (2nd Temple).

The sages who learned from Hillel and Shammai, and continued to discuss their teachings, were called the *Tannaim*, which means "Repeaters" of the *Torah Shebaal Peh* (Oral Torah). The *Tannaim* sat for five generations after the *Zuggot*.

Hillel & Shammai: On One Foot

There is an account recorded in the Talmud (Shabbat 31a) of a man that came to the Zuggot, Hillel and Shammai. He first went to Shammai, the more stringent of the pair, and said that he would accept Judaism if Shammai could teach him the entire Torah while he stood on one foot. Insulted with this ridiculous request, Shammai sent him away.

The man did not give up, so he went to Hillel who was known to be a very patient and humble man who taught his students, "love peace and pursue peace, love all G-d's creations and bring them close to the Torah."

When the man asked Hillel to teach him the entire Torah while he stood on one foot. Hillel replied, *"What is hateful to you, do not do to your neighbor. That is the whole Torah; the rest is the explanation of this—go and study it!"*

TRUE or FALSE?

1. The *Anshei K'nesset Hagedolah* (Men of the Great Assembly) first convened during the Babylonian Exile, and led the people in righteousness into the Second Temple Period.

2. The Greater Sanhedrin is made up of 70 members.

3. Over the course of 120 years, there were 100 men who participated in the *Anshei K'nesset Hagedolah*.

4. The following men were all members of the *Anshei K'nesset Hagedolah:* Haggai, Zechariah, Malachi, Mordechai, Daniel, Ezra, and Nehamiah.

5. The *Anshei K'Nesset Hagedolah* formalized the prayer services, established synagogues, organized the *Torah Shebaal Peh* into tractates, enacted rabbinic decrees, and designated the books of the *Tenakh* as Scripture.

6. Rabbinic decrees are additions to the *mitzvot* of the Torah.

7. The pair of men that led the Sanhedrin for 250 years were called *Zuggot.*

8. The leader of the Sanhedrin that oversees the teaching is called the *Nasi.*

9. The leader of the Sanhedrin that oversees the court of law is called the *Av Beit Din.*

10. Hillel and Shammai were not the last pair of *Zuggot.*

11. The *Tannaim* "Repeaters" were taught by the *Zuggot* and sat as leaders for five generations.

ANSWERS

1. TRUE

2. TRUE

3. FALSE

4. TRUE

5. TRUE

6. FALSE

7. TRUE

8. TRUE

9. TRUE

10. FALSE

11. TRUE

MISHNAH

REBBI YEHUDA HANASI GATHERED the *Torah Shebaal Peh* (Oral Torah) from the sages and organized it into a book called The *Mishnah*, which comes from the root word *shenah*, "to repeat." Once Rebbi Yehuda HaNasi (descendent of Hillel) completed the *Mishnah* in 200CE, it was accepted by the Sages and closed so that nobody could add to or take away from it.

Rabbi Yehuda was the last of the *Tannaim*, and was also referred to as *Rabbeinu HaKodosh*, "our saintly teacher." Many simply called him "Rabbi," because he was so famous that no other name was needed to identify him. The Talmud tells us that from the time of Moses to Rabbi Yehudah, no other individual embodied in himself supreme greatness in Torah scholarship, wealth, and political power.

Rabbi was fond of saying, "I have learned much from my teachers, even more from my friends and fellow students, but most of all I learned from my pupils."

The compilation of the Mishnah is especially remarkable because it was forbidden for a public record of the Oral Torah to be written before Rabbi Yehudah. Why was it prohibited?

Writing it down would (1) limit its scope, (2) its intricacies and practicalities can't be completely learned merely from text alone, and (3) it could be claimed by others as their own saying they are the chosen Jewish people.

Rabbi Yehuda convened all Torah scholars in the land of Israel over many years in the midst of dire times of persecution to compile the *Mishnah*.

The *Mishnah* has six sections called *sidarim*, meaning "orders." This made it easier to be memorized, especially during that time of great persecution and dispersion to foreign lands. The six *sidarim* are broken down into 63 tractates, 525 chapters, and 4,224 *Mishnayot*.

These are the six *sidarim* of the *Mishnah*:

1) *Zeraim* (Seeds) pertains to everything regarding food, even planting, harvesting, and blessings.

2) *Moed* (Set Feasts) pertains to Shabbat, holidays, and fast days.

3) *Nashim* (Women) pertains to marriage and divorce.

4) *Nezikin* (Damages) pertains to money, property, and harm done to others.

5) *Kodashim* (Holy Things) pertains to sacrifices and kosher.

6) *Tohoroth* (Cleannesses) pertains to spiritual cleanliness and purity.

Each of the *sidarim* are organized into sections called *mesechtot*, which means "woven," because the *mesechtot* are all connected together. Within the *mesechtot* are chapters, and each chapter is called a *perekh*.

The least to the greatest of all the people of the earth have benefitted immensely from the life of Rabbi Yehudah and the completion of the Mishnah. Rabbi was so influential and revered by all people that Emperor Antoninus of Rome openly sought wisdom of the Torah from him on a regular basis. There are many stories in the Talmud about Rabbi's many great deeds.

Rabbi Yehudah: Body & Soul

Once Antoninus asked Rabbi: "How can the human soul be punished in the next world? The soul will be able to say: 'How can I be held to blame? I am a spiritual creation. It was the body that sinned, not I.' On the other hand, the body will be able to say: 'How can I be guilty? Without the soul I could not have sinned, for it is the soul which gives life to the body.'"

To this question of the Emperor, "Rabbi" replied with a clever parable (example):

A man once owned an orchard, over which he set two servants to guard it. One of the watchers was blind; the other was lame: The lame man, tempted by the sight of the ripe fruit which he could not reach, said to his blind companion: "Carry me on your shoulders and lead me to that tree, laden with rich fruit, to which I shall guide you. In this way both of us will enjoy the fruit"

When the owner, noticing the loss of his fruit, later accused his two servants of the theft of his choicest fruit, the blind man protested his innocence. "How could I have seen where the fruit was growing?" And the lame servant said: "How could I have reached the fruit?"

How did the owner act? He placed the lame man on the shoulders of the blind man and then punished them together.

So, too, replied the Rabbi, does G-d with the human body and soul when each falsely tries to avoid punishment for its guilt.

This is proof that the body will be resurrected, and reanimated by the soul, to be judged. However, this parable also explains the relationship of the Written Torah and Oral Torah. The Written Torah is like a body, a vessel that is unable to function to accomplish a task without the animation of the Oral Torah. How could we do what is written in the Torah without receiving the oral instruction of how to do it?

"Make *tzitzit* on the corners of your garment, with a cord of *techelet* on each *tzitzit" (Numbers 15:38)*. What are *tzitzit?* What is *techelet?* What do they look like? How do we make them? Who can make them? How are they attached? What kind of garment are they attached to?

And you shall bind them as a sign upon your hand, and as *tefillin* between your eyes" (Deuteronomy 6:8). What are *tefillin?* What do they look like? When do we put them on? Who puts them on?

Many people have tried to invent their own definitions of what the words of the Written Torah mean and how to perform them, but without the Oral Torah these attempts are worse than an empty body that is unable to accomplish a task. Rather, it is like the lame man guiding the blind man to steal the choicest fruit from HaShem, the Master of the Garden.

The Torah is precious to HaShem, and it is not something to be used however we see fit. With the same amount of effort, these two thieves could have received the fruit from the master and eat of it in joy, but they chose to attain it according to their own understanding.

TRUE or FALSE?

1. The *Mishnah* was compiled by Rebbi Yehudah HaNasi.
2. The *Mishnah* was completed in 2000CE.
3. The six sections (sidarim) of the *Mishnah* are *Zeraim, Moed, Nashim, Nezekin, Kodashim,* and *Tohoroth.*
4. *Zeraim* means "Seeds."
5. *Moed* means "Additional Education."
6. *Nashim* means "Women."
7. *Nezikin* means "Damages."
8. *Kodashim* means "Holy Things."
9. *Tohoroth* means "Torah Things."
10. *Sidarim* are made up of divisions called *mesechtot.*
11. *Mesechtot* are made up of divisions called a *perekh.*

ANSWERS

1. TRUE

2. FALSE

3. TRUE

4. TRUE

5. FALSE

6. TRUE

7. TRUE

8. TRUE

9. FALSE

10. TRUE

11. TRUE

GEMARAH & TALMUD

*A*FTER THE FIVE GENERATIONS of *Zuggot* and the five generations of *Tannaim*, the next seven generations of sages were called the *Ammoraim*, which means "explainers" or "speakers," and they taught The Mishnah to the people of Israel. For hundreds of years the *Ammoraim* discussed the *Mishnah*, and each of these discussions is called a *Suggiah*. All of the *suggiot* collected together are called the *Gemarah*, "the teaching."

The *Mishnah* and the *Gemarah* were integrated together and called the *Talmud*, which also means "the teaching," and each book of the *Talmud* is often referred to as a *Gemarah* even though it contains the *Mishnah* and the *Gemarah*.

When the Babylonian King Nebukadnetstsar destroyed the *1st Beit HaMikdash* (Temple), the Jews were taken into captivity to the land of Babylon. From the time of the Babylonian captivity until after the time of the *Tannaim*, there remained a vibrant Jewish community within the nation of Babylon. After the 2nd *Beit HaMikdash* was destroyed by the Romans, the Jews in Israel were very restricted in their ability to learn and teach the Torah in the land of Israel.

In fact, the Jews were forced out of Jerusalem and resided in northern Israel. However, the Jews that lived in Babylon were not hindered in this way. They had houses of Torah learning there called *yeshivot,* just like they did in Israel, and each *yeshiva* is a crucial part of Jewish learning even to this very day all over the world.

That is why there is a *Talmud Yerushalami* (Jerusalem Talmud) and a *Talmud Bevli* (Babylonian Talmud). The *Mishnah* within both is the same, and the *Talmud Bevli* contains the *Gemarah* of the *Talmud Yerushalami.*

However, the *Talmud Bevli* has additional *Gemarah* from the rest of the *Ammoriam* that were allowed to discuss the *Mishnah* more freely within the borders of Babylon. For this reason, the *Talmud Bevli* is simply referred to as the *Talmud*, because it contains both the *Talmud Yerushalami* and the *Talmud Bevli.*

Moshe Rabbeinu & Rabbi Akiva

Of all the great sages, Rabbi Akiva stands out as one of the greatest. Rabbi Yehuda HaNassi, compiler of the Mishnah, relied heavily upon Rabbi Akiva's writings. When reading the Mishnah, it seems as if Rabbi Akiva is quoted on every page. Much of the Gemarah is discussion on the text that Rabbi Akiva inherited from Moses our teacher.

The Talmud relates the passing down of the Torah with an interesting story.

Moses ascended Mt. Sinai to receive the Torah. He found the Holy One, blessed is He, sitting and attaching crowns to the letters of the Torah. (It's important to note here that this is an allegorical expression, as HaShem has no bodily form.)

Moses, not seeing a need for the crowns, asked, "Master of the Universe! Who forces You to go to such extremes?"

G-d answered, "There is a man who will live many generations after you and his name is Akiva, son of Yosef. He will examine every single spike of every letter and draw from them piles upon piles of *halachot*."

So Moses asked, "Master of the Universe! Show him to me!"

G-d replied, "Step backwards."

And Moses stepped back until he found himself standing in the 18th row of Rabbi Akiva's class. You see, the students were arranged in this class by order of their understanding. It seems the only thing left after the eighteenth row was out in the hallway.

So Moses stood there and listened—and was unable to follow a thing that was said. He became weak with despair. Until finally, a ruling came up for which Rabbi Akiva could provide no source. A student asked of Rabbi Akiva, "Where do you learn this from?"

Rabbi Akiva responded, "This is an oral tradition passed down from Moses."

By those words, Moses was set at ease.

When Moses heard Rabbi Akiva teaching, he was concerned because he did not know for certain that this was the Torah as Rabbi

Akiva had received it. But once he heard that this man was not one to take credit for himself, but rather to quote in Moses' name, he understood that Rabbi Akiva's teachings were pure, unadulterated Torah, the same Torah Moses was to receive, only unfolded and unpacked.

TRUE or FALSE?

1. The *Zuggot* sat for five generations, *Tannaim* sat for five generations, and the *Ammoriam* sat for seven generations.

2. The *Ammoriam* did not explain or speak the *Mishnah* to the people.

3. Each discussion of the *Mishnah* is called a *suggiah*.

4. All of the *suggiot* together are called the *Gemarah,* which means "the teaching."

5. The *Talmud* contains the *Mishnah* but not the *Gemarah.*

6. *Talmud* means "the teaching."

7. Nebukadnetstsar was the king of Assyria that destroyed the 1ˢᵗ *Beit HaMikdash* and took Israel into captivity.

8. The Romans destroyed the 2ⁿᵈ *Beit HaMikdash.*

9. After the 2ⁿᵈ *Beit HaMikdash* was destroyed, the Jews in Babylon had more freedom to learn the Torah than in the Roman controlled land of Israel.

10. The *Talmud Bevli* was written by Babylonians.

11. The *Talmud Bevli* contains everything that is in the *Talmud Yerushalami.*

12. There is a different *Mishnah* in the *Talmud Bevli* than the *Talmud Yerushalami.*

13. The *Talmud Bevli* contains additional *Gemarah* that are not found in the *Talmud Yerushalami* due to Roman oppression in Israel.

14. When someone says *"Talmud,"* they are referring to the *Talmud Bevli.*

ANSWERS

1. TRUE

2. FALSE

3. TRUE

4. TRUE

5. FALSE

6. TRUE

7. FALSE

8. TRUE

9. TRUE

10. FALSE

11. TRUE

12. FALSE

13. TRUE

14. TRUE

POST-TALMUDIC SCHOLARSHIP

*A*FTER THE TALMUD WAS COMPLETED in 500CE, the *Geonim* carried the torch of teaching the *Talmud* for several hundred years. *Geon* means "genius."

After the *Geonim*, the leaders were called the *Rishonim*, "the first ones." They taught from 1,000--1,500CE. Two of the most notable *Rishonim* are Rashi and Rambam.

Rashi

Rabbi Shlomo Yitzhaki, also referred to by the acronym Rashi, was an 11th century French rabbi and *Talmud* commentator. After the printing press was invented, it became the standard practice to have Rashi's commentary, along with the commentary of other Jewish scholars compiled by Rashi, right on the page alongside the Mishnah and Gemarah.

One year before Rashi's birth, his father, Rabbi Yitzchak found a rare diamond. "Now, there would be no more poverty," he thought and went to sell the precious stone to the local jeweler. The jeweler hadn't enough money to pay for such a large diamond, and suggested to the bishop to buy it.

The bishop had been looking for such a diamond for he wanted to put it on his cross. He offered a huge amount of money for it. When Rabbi Yitzchak heard for what purpose the bishop wanted the stone, he refused to sell it. He knew, however, that if he did not sell the stone, it would be taken from him forcibly, so he threw it into the sea.

A Heavenly Voice then resounded: "For this great sacrifice you will be blessed with a son that will outshine all the precious stones in the world, and the light of his Torah will shine forever."

The following year a son was born to him, and he called him Solomon, saying, may G-d grant him wisdom like unto King Solomon. And indeed, Rashi most definitely lived up to his name.

Rambam

Rabbi Moshe ben Maimon, or Maimonides, is known by the acronym Rambam, and is a descendent of Rabbi Yehudah HaNassi (descendant of King David). Because of his great contributions to Judaism, some refer to Rambam as "the second Moses." Rambam's gravestone reads, "From Moses to Moses, none arose as Moses."

Rambam's mother died while giving birth to him. His father was the Beit Din, the chief rabbi of that time. Moshe was learning disabled, unable to learn or retain any knowledge. When he was six years old, he attended the evening prayer service, and he stayed there all night crying.

In the middle of that night he had a vision. He saw sparks of red and gold, and his head was laid open, like an open mind. Then Moshe picked up a page of Torah, and he all of a sudden understood it all. He recognized that he had instantly become a genius with a photographic memory.

Moshe didn't tell his father about what happened because he didn't know how long this genius mind of his would last. His father's teacher, Rabbi Yosef Ibn Meir Ha-Levi Ibn Megas, didn't know who Moshe was, so he left home and began studying under Rabbi Megas.

After a few months of study, the Rabbi was about to pass away. Moshe embraced his hand and kissed it. At that moment, all of the wisdom of Rabbi Megas was transferred to Moshe. After Rabbi Megas passed away, Moshe returned home to Kordoba, Spain and approached the bima at the front of the synagogue on Shabbat and began reading the Torah, all of this at six years old.

Rambam's father asked, "Who is this child?" They replied, "This is your son who ran away!" At that moment Rambam was recognized publicly as a child prodigy, and he became close with his father as a son and a student.

Rambam was a 12th century Sephardic Jewish Torah scholar, philosopher, and even became the head physician of the renowned Saladin, sultan of Egypt and Syria. His most notable writings are the philosophical work: *Guide for the Perplexed,* and the first index of the entire body of the Oral Law: *Mishnah Torah.*

Rambam undertook the huge task of writing *Mishnah Torah* in order to condense down into one practical work the incredible volume of knowledge contained in the *Talmud,* the explanations of the *Geonim,* and the commentaries of the *Rishonim.* Rambam alludes to this in the introduction to his amazing fourteen volume work.

To summarize: [The intent of this text is] that a person will not need another text at all with regard to any Jewish law. Rather, this text will be a compilation of the entire Oral Law, including also the ordinances, customs, and decrees that were enacted from the time of Moses, our teacher, until the completion of the Talmud, as were explained by the Geonim in the texts they composed after the Talmud.

Therefore, I have called this text, Mishnah Torah ["the second to the Torah," with the intent that] a person should first study the Written Law, and then study this text and comprehend the entire Oral Law from it, without having to study any other text between the two.

I saw fit to divide this text into [separate] halachot pertaining to each [particular] subject, and, within the context of a single subject, to divide those halachot into chapters. Each and every chapter is divided into smaller halachot so that they can be ordered in one's memory.

Due to the wisdom of Torah and the genius mind that HaShem gave to Rambam, he was the first in history to accomplish this task. To this very day, Orthodox Judaism as a whole holds *Mishnah Torah* in high esteem as one of the greatest works of Torah scholarship of all time.

Rabbi Yoseph Karo

After the *Rishonim,* Rabbi Yoseph Karo authored the Code of Jewish Law called the *Shulchan Aruch,* or "Set Table." Rabbi Karo finished writing *Shulchan Aruch* after he moved to Israel, and it was published in 1565CE.

When the leading sage of Tsfat, Israel passed away, Rabbi Karo was regarded as his successor. He and Rabbi Moshe of Trani (the Mabit) headed the Rabbinical Court of Tsfat. By this time, the Rabbinical Court of Tsfat had become the central rabbinical court in all of Israel and the entire *Diaspora*.

There was not a single matter of national or global importance that did not come to the attention and ruling of the Tsfat *Beit Din*. Its rulings were accepted as final and conclusive. Rabbi Karo's *halachic* decisions and clarifications were sought by sages from every corner of the *Diaspora*, and he came to be regarded as the leader of the entire generation.

Rabbi Karo's *Shulchan Aruch* is the most widely used compilation of *halacha* (Jewish law) ever written. It contains four sections:

1) *Orach Chayim* pertains to laws
   of prayer and synagogue, Sabbath, and holidays.
2) *Yoreh De'ah* pertains to laws of kashrut, religious conversion,
   mourning, laws pertaining to Israel, and laws of family purity.
3) *Even Ha'ezer* pertains to laws of marriage, divorce, and related
   issues.
4) *Choshen Mishpat* pertains to laws of finance, financial
   responsibility, damages (personal and financial), and the rules of
   the Beit Din, as well as the laws of witnesses.

Romm Publishing House

The formatting of the printed *Talmud* was standardized in 1886CE when the *Talmud* was printed in Vilna, Lithuania by the Romm publishing house. Now, every page number of the *Talmud* is the same, and every line on each page begins and ends in the same place. This allows Jews today to study *Talmud* much more efficiently all over the world.

TRUE or FALSE?

1. The *Talmud* was completed in 500CE.
2. The *Geonim* taught the *Talmud* for hundreds of years until the *Rishonim*.
3. The *Rishonim* taught from 1000-1500CE.
4. Rashi is an acronym for Rabbi Shlomo Yitzhaki, the 11th century French Rabbi and *Talmud* commentator.
5. Rashi's commentary does not appear in the most common copies of the *Talmud*.
6. Rambam is an acronym for Rabbi Moshe ben Maimon, or Maimonides.
7. Rambam was a 12th century Ashkenazi Jewish philosopher.
8. Rambam was born after *Mishnah Torah* was written in the 12th century.
9. *Mishnah Torah* was written with the intent that a person would need no other text at all in regards to Jewish Law.
10. Rabbi Joseph Karo authored *Shulchan Aruch,* and it was published in 1565CE.
11. *Shulchan Aruch* contains five sections: *Orach Chayim, Yoreh De'ah, Even Ha'ezer, Choshen Mishpat,* and *Bereishit*.
12. Romm publishing house standardized the printing of the *Talmud* in 1886BCE.

ANSWERS

1. TRUE
2. TRUE
3. TRUE
4. TRUE
5. FALSE
6. TRUE
7. FALSE
8. FALSE
9. TRUE
10. TRUE
11. FALSE
12. FALSE

INTERPRETATION

THERE ARE FOUR methods by which the Torah can be interpreted, referred to by the acronym PaRDeS *(pardes)*. *Pardes* stands for *peshat*, *remez*, *derash*, and *sod*.

Peshat: "Straight" refers to the literal meaning of the text.

Remez: "Hint" refers to the hidden or allegorical meaning behind the literal reading of the text.

Derash: "Inquire" is derived by comparing other similar occurrences in the text.

Sod: "Mystery" or "secret" refers to the mystical meaning of the text.

These four ways of understanding of the Torah are sewn into the fabric of the text. They are not subjective to the individual's opinion; rather, the *pardes* of the text is an intrinsic part of the Torah itself and can be understood with the proper approach by a kosher Torah teacher.

All four aspects of Torah study are dependent upon one another. If any piece is removed, the meaning is incomplete. For instance, if one studies the Zohar (*sod* level), yet does not even have a firm grasp on *peshat*, it is impossible to understand correctly and leads to much corruption and destruction.

What good is a garment if one never learns to don it properly? He carries it around day and night, examines each thread, shows his friends how intricate and beautiful it is, revels in its workmanship, uses it as a centerpiece to regale his guests at great banquets, hangs it up in a prominent place in his home, and displays it as a banner at his gates; yet he remains naked because he never gained proper understanding and application. How shameful!

For this reason it is crucial to learn Torah from kosher Orthodox sources. If one simply interprets the Torah according to his own opinions or improper approach, he will end up with the wrong interpretation that was never intended. This is dangerous and leads to inventing one's own religion, which we will cover in upcoming chapters.

The Torah applied to one's life properly leads to character development and proper conduct in every facet of one's life. It is not meant to be purely for intellectual ascent. One who studies day and night to gain proper understanding but never develops in maturity is also like the naked man carrying around a beautiful garment day and night.

We should learn from kosher Orthodox sources that are operating under the proper authority in their role as a Torah teacher. This does not mean we shouldn't read the text and find meaning. It's actually quite the opposite!

We learn from the Torah knowing that there is a proper understanding and application, and we should verify it with kosher Torah learning, rather than projecting our own assumptions upon the holy text, as if to convince ourselves that we speak on behalf of HaShem and arrogantly define what he "really" meant when He said "such and such."

In Judaism, opinions are not Torah. Personal interpretation is not Torah. Rather than forming our thoughts into opinions, which are conclusions reached internally, we should form our thoughts in the shape of questions. He who asks the most questions gains the most wisdom.

Torah and all of its understanding is passed down, inherited, not invented, and there are definite answers. Until a person realizes that his own mind and heart are not the source of wisdom to understand what his eyes see, he is unable to gain proper understanding.

Many claim to have revelations from G-d, but it is their own imagination, and you are not special in this regard. If you want to learn Torah, you must use your mind to adopt proper understanding from proper sources, not invent your own understanding from the source of your own mind.

We do not derive knowledge from our own heart. Rather, we are instructed to inscribe the love and faithfulness we have inherited from HaShem onto our hearts and lean not on our own understanding. It is

better to consult with a rabbi than to be led astray by one's own heart
and invent one's own religion.

> *My son, do not forget my teaching,*
> *but keep my commandments in your heart,*
> *for they will prolong your life many years*
> *and bring you peace and prosperity.*
> *Let love and faithfulness never leave you;*
> *bind them around your neck,*
> *write them on the tablet of your heart.*
> *Then you will win favor and a good name*
> *in the sight of G-d and man.*
> *Trust in HaShem with all your heart*
> *and lean not on your own understanding;*
> *in all your ways submit to him,*
> *and he will make your paths straight.*
> *Do not be wise in your own eyes;*
> *fear HaShem and shun evil.*
> *This will bring health to your body*
> *and nourishment to your bones.*

Proverbs 3:1-8

Rabbi Yonatan: Following the Majority

The great Rabbi Yonatan Eibenschutz (1690-1764CE) was the
leader of the famed "Three Communities" in Germany. When he was
just three years old he was so famous for his wisdom that the king of
Poland heard about him and decided to put the child prodigy to the
test.

The king sent a message to little Yonatan's father instructing
him to send his son to the royal palace unassisted to see if the

boy could find his way through the several miles of confusing city streets.

The next day he dressed the boy in his best Shabbat clothes, blessed him, and sent him off, hoping for the best. Several hours later he arrived at the palace.

The guards couldn't believe their eyes and ears when the little boy presented himself proudly before them and announced in a high-pitched voice that he had come to see the king.

Little Yonatan was taken before the king's court, and the king spoke, "Tell me, my boy, how did you find your way to the palace?"

"Well, your majesty," he answered, "whenever I had a doubt I just asked anyone that happened to be nearby, and it seems that G-d helped."

The king responded, "But didn't it ever occur to you that two people might say opposite things? What if one said to go to the right, and the other to the left? What would you have done then?"

"Your majesty, in the Torah it says that when faced with differing opinions, one should follow the majority. That's what I would have done—I'd have asked a third person and followed the majority opinion."

The king moved forward on his throne, gazed piercingly at the boy, and said, "Young man, you should listen to what you yourself just said! If in your Bible it says you must follow the majority, then certainly you should forsake Judaism and believe as we do, as we are the majority!"

"Pardon me, your royal highness. When I said that I would follow the majority, I meant when I was far from the castle and uncertain of the location. But now that I'm *in* the castle and I see the king seated before me, even if *all* the king's ministers tell me I'm in the wrong place, I will certainly not listen to them.

"The G-d of Israel is everywhere, and no place is empty of Him. It is like being in the palace with the king. Even if the entire world disagrees with me, I certainly have no reason to listen to them!"

TRUE or FALSE?

1. Pardes is an acronym for peshat, remez, derash, and sod.
2. Peshat is the literal meaning of the text.
3. Remez is the hidden/allegorical meaning of the text.
4. Derash is the meaning derived by sharing opinions.
5. Sod is the mystical meaning of the text.
6. Orthodox Judaism teaches the correct interpretation of the Torah.
7. Interpreting the Torah according to one's own understanding leads to creating one's own religion.
8. Non-Jews should not read the Torah.

ANSWERS

1. TRUE
2. TRUE
3. TRUE
4. FALSE
5. TRUE
6. TRUE
7. TRUE
8. FALSE

TORAH
FOR THE
NATIONS

IN ALL, THERE ARE 613 INSTRUCTIONS of the Torah called *mitzvot.* Each *mitzvah* is a commandment from HaShem that was given to the Jewish people through Moses at Mount Sinai for the purpose of bringing light into the whole world through the Jewish people.

Positive *mitzvot* are instructions to "do," and negative *mitzvot* are instructions to "do not." There are 248 positive *mitzvot* pertaining to the number of members that make up the human body, and 365 negative *mitzvot* pertaining to the number of days in the solar year.

The 613 commandments are obligatory to all Jews because all of the Jews stood at Mount Sinai and said in a unified voice,

"We will do everything HaShem has said" (Shemot/Exodus 19:8).

However, not all of the *mitzvot* can be done by one person. Why?

The 613 commandments were received by the Jewish people as a nation. There are many different roles people hold in the nation, and without each other the nation could not accomplish doing all 613 commandments they agreed to at Mt. Sinai.

For example there are *mitzvot* that only women can do, some only men can do, and others only a *kohen* (priest) can do. There are *mitzvot* for high priests, kings, butchers, leapers, farmers, children, parents, homeowners, etc. There are *mitzvot* that can only be done in the Land of Israel, when the Temple is standing, when a non-Jew lives amongst Jews, or only when your brother dies and leaves a widow.

The point is that the 613 *mitzvot* can't all be done by one person, and that's why it's so important for each individual to do their part. Otherwise the nation of Israel can't fulfill its role, and the light of the Torah will not go out to the nations.

If you've gotten this far through the book, there's a good chance you have a strong desire to connect more deeply with HaShem through the light of Torah Judaism. *Baruch HaShem!*

If you're a non-Jew, you're probably wondering what Judaism teaches about your relationship with the Torah since your ancestors did not stand at Mt. Sinai and enter into the covenant between HaShem and Israel.

The ancient Jewish teachers say that HaShem went to each nation and asked them to enter into a covenant with Him, and every nation asked questions about the terms of the covenant. The Jewish people were the only nation that said "I do" without asking questions. This gives us some insight into why HaShem entrusted the Torah and the 613 *mitzvot* to the Jews.

And even with such a painful history of extreme persecution and suffering, the Jews have preserved and practiced the same Torah without adding or subtracting even one letter for over 3,300 years.

That's amazing!

Are non-Jews required to keep Torah?

(Mishnah Torah, Melachim uMilchamot 8:10)

Moses only gave the Torah and mitzvot as an inheritance to Israel, as Deuteronomy 33:4 states: 'The Torah... is the inheritance of the congregation of Jacob,' and to all those who desire to convert from among the other nations, as Numbers 15:15 states 'the convert shall be the same as you.' However, someone who does not desire to accept Torah and mitzvot, should not be forced to.

By the same regard, Moses was commanded by the Almighty to compel all the inhabitants of the world to accept the commandments given to Noah's descendants.

The short of it is that non-Jews are NOT required to keep the 613 commandments because they've never taken on that yoke by entering into the covenant at Mt. Sinai. The only way for the non-Jew to be obligated to keep all 613 commandments is to convert to Judaism.

However, that doesn't mean non-Jews can't do any of the *mitzvot*, nor that they shouldn't. In fact there are seven laws in the Torah that every human being alive today is obligated to observe.

The Covenant with Noah

"Then G-d said to Noah and to his sons with him: 'I now establish my covenant with you and with your descendants after you'" (Genesis 9:8-9).

Since every person alive today is a descendant of Noah, the covenant of Noah applies to all people, even Jews. In fact, the seven laws given to Noah are included in the 613 commandments of the Torah given to the Jews at Mt. Sinai.

So, as a non-Jew are you required to keep the Torah? Yes and no. You're required to keep the *mitzvot* of the Torah that apply to you as a non-Jew, which are the Seven Laws of Noah, just like each individual within the Jewish people does his or her part according to their role.

Non-Jews are not obligated to do all 613 *mitzvot* of the Torah... and neither is any individual Jew as we discussed earlier. Each human being on the earth is required to do everything in accordance to the established covenants in the Torah that apply to them within their role.

What is a Bnei Noach or Noahide?

A non-Jew that keeps the seven laws of Noah with the intent of serving HaShem is called a *Bnei Noach* or a *Noahide*. The ancient Jewish sages teach that a Non-Jew who abides by the Noahide Laws is a righteous gentile and has a place in *olam haba* (the world to come). There's even a teaching that the righteousness of the righteous gentile is like that of the *Kohen HaGadol* (High Priest).

(Mishnah Torah, Melachim uMilchamot 8:11)

"Anyone who accepts upon himself the fulfillment of these seven mitzvot and is precise in their observance is considered one of 'the pious among the gentiles' and will merit a share in the world to come.

This applies only when he accepts them and fulfills them because the Holy One, blessed be He, commanded them in the Torah and informed us through Moses, our teacher, that Noah's descendants had been commanded to fulfill them previously.

However, if he fulfills them out of intellectual conviction, he is not a resident alien, nor of 'the pious among the gentiles,' nor of their wise men."

Can I do *mitzvot?*

What you're about to hear may shock you, but please don't jump to conclusions too quickly. Here's what the renowned Jewish scholar Rambam said about the seven laws of Noah in *Mishnah Torah.*

(Melachim uMilchamot 10:9-10)

A gentile who studies the Torah is obligated to die. They should only be involved in the study of their seven mitzvot.

Similarly, a gentile who rests, even on a weekday, observing that day as a Sabbath, is obligated to die. Needless to say, he is obligated for that punishment if he creates a festival for himself.

The general principle governing these matters is: They are not to be allowed to originate a new religion or create mitzvot for themselves based on their own decisions. They may either become righteous converts and accept all the mitzvot or retain their statutes without adding or detracting from them.

If a gentile studies the Torah, makes a Sabbath, or creates a religious practice, a Jewish court should beat him, punish him, and inform him that he is obligated to die. However, he is not to be executed."

We should not prevent a gentile who desires to perform one of the Torah's mitzvot in order to receive reward from doing so, provided he performs it as required. If he brings an animal to be sacrificed as a burnt offering, we should receive it.

What is Rambam saying here? Is any non-Jew that picks up a Torah and reads it obligated to die? Of course not! If a non-Jew studies the Torah and decides they want to do a *mitzvah* in a manner

NOT prescribed by *halacha* (Jewish Law), this is considered creating one's own *mitzvah* and religion.

It is strictly prohibited to add to or take away from the *mitzvot* of the Torah. However, Rambam says if a non-Jew wants to perform one of the *mitzvot* in accordance with Jewish law, he should not be prevented.

Shemayah & Avtalion: Converts Teaching Hillel

Shemayah and Avtalion were the leaders of the Sanhedrin, number thirteen on the list of the forty generations of transmission of the Torah. They were both righteous converts to Judaism. Hillel, who sits at number twelve (in descending order), received it from Shemayah and Avtalion.

When Hillel sat as a student under Shemayah and Avtalion, he was a poor man chopping wood, earning only enough to provide food for his family and pay the guard for entry into the house of study.

It was the eve of Shabbat in the winter solstice, and Hillel did not have the very small amount (a half coin) to pay the guard for entry to hear Shemayah and Avtalion teach. So, Hillel climbed up onto the roof and peered in through a window.

Throughout the night a heavy snow fell down upon him. When the sun rose, Shemayah said to Avtalyon, 'Every day this house is light and today it is dark; is it perhaps a cloudy day?' They looked up and saw the figure of a man in the window.

They went up and found Hillel covered by three cubits (4.5 feet) of snow. They removed him, bathed and anointed him, and placed him opposite the fire, and they said, 'This man deserves that the Shabbat be profaned on his behalf.'"

A person who desires to learn Torah must not be bashful. The Torah has wisdom for all people, whether a native born Jew, a convert, or a non-Jew from the nations. From the poorest to the wealthiest, one who is not bashful in his pursuit of Torah will be helped.

TRUE or FALSE

1. There are 613 *mitzvot* of the Torah.

2. The *mitzvot* were given to the Jewish people at Mt. Sinai.

3. All Jews are obligated to keep the *mitzvot*.

4. All of the *mitzvot* can be performed by one person.

5. Each person should do the *mitzvot* that apply to their role in the world.

6. The Torah and *mitzvot* were only given as an inheritance to the congregation of Jacob and those who convert to the congregation of Jacob and accept the Torah and *mitzvot* as prescribed by the congregation of Jacob.

7. Non-Jews are required to keep the 613 *mitzvot*.

8. Jews and Non-Jews are required to keep the seven laws of the covenant of Noah.

9. One can be a righteous gentile if he does the Seven unintentionally out of intellectual conviction.

10. Righteous gentiles (*Noahides*) have a place in *olam haba* (the world to come).

11. The righteousness of the righteous gentile can't compare to the righteousness of the High Priest.

12. An idolater that studies the Torah is obligated to die. (continue...)

13. A gentile who redefines for themselves any *mitzvah* of the Torah in a way that was not explained to Moses at Mt. Sinai

has created his own *mitzvah* and religion and is obligated to die.

14. Non-Jews should not be prevented from performing the Torah's *mitzvot* in the proper *halachic* manner.

ANSWERS

1. TRUE

2. TRUE

3. TRUE

4. FALSE

5. TRUE

6. TRUE

7. FALSE

8. TRUE

9. FALSE

10. TRUE

11. FALSE

12. TRUE

13. TRUE

14. TRUE

NOAHIDE
LAWS

S O, YOU HAVE TO BE WONDERING by now what the
seven laws of Noah are. This chapter is composed as an
introduction to the Seven. The non-Jew should devote
himself to the study and practice of the Seven.

This is an overview for the purpose of giving the reader a
kosher introduction to these subjects on which one can pursue a
lifetime of learning and good deeds on the righteous path.

Who can find the end of learning and understanding? For this
reason, this chapter is considerably short, but will give the reader
enough information to take monumental steps in the path of a
righteous gentile.

The first six of the Seven Laws were actually given to Adam,
and a seventh was added at the time of Noah.

> *(Mishnah Torah, Melachim uMilchamot 9:1)*
> *Six precepts were commanded to Adam:*
>   *1) the prohibition against worship of false gods;*
>   *2) the prohibition against cursing G-d;*
>   *3) the prohibition against murder;*
>   *4) the prohibition against incest and adultery;*
>   *5) the prohibition against theft;*
>   *6) the command to establish laws and courts of justice.*
>
> *Even though we have received all of these commands from Moses and, furthermore, they are concepts which intellect itself tends to accept, it appears from the Torah's words that Adam was commanded concerning them.*
>
>   *7) The prohibition against eating flesh from a living animal was added for Noah, as Genesis 9:4 states: 'Nevertheless, you may not eat flesh with its life, which is its blood.' Thus there are seven mitzvot."*

Let's stop here for just a moment and reemphasize that each of these commandments must be defined and practiced in the prescribed manner as defined in Jewish Law. If you decide for yourself how to define "worship of false gods" according to your own reasoning apart from Jewish Law, you are creating your own *mitzvah* and your own religion. It is imperative to learn what Torah Judaism teaches about these seven laws.

It is important to remember that the Jews were chosen to carry the light of the Torah to all the nations. Think about this... If the Jewish people were not carrying the torch of the Torah today, the non-Jew wouldn't even know how to begin serving the G-d of the universe, let alone how to be a righteous person.

Thus, it is necessary for the Noahide to acknowledge the validity and preservation of the Written Torah and the *Torah Shebaal Peh*

(Oral Torah). Otherwise he would be creating another religion, even though his intentions and tenacity may be admirable. The Seven must be studied and practiced by the Noahide in accordance with what Orthodox Judaism teaches.

Now we're going to get a little deeper into the seven Laws of Noah with Rambam from the text of *Mishnah Torah.*

1) The prohibition against worship of false gods.

(Melachim uMilchamot 9:2)

A gentile who worships false gods is liable provided he worships them in an accepted manner.

A gentile is executed for every type of foreign worship which a Jewish court would consider worthy of capital punishment. However, a gentile is not executed for a type of foreign worship which a Jewish court would not deem worthy of capital punishment. Nevertheless, even though a gentile will not be executed for these forms of worship, he is forbidden to engage in all of them.

We should not allow them to erect a monument, or to plant an Asherah, or to make images and the like even though they are only for the sake of beauty.

It is prohibited to worship false gods, so we must understand what constitutes as a false god. Therefore, we must understand what the one true G-d is and what He isn't. Anyone who worships an entity that deviates even slightly from the following definition of G-d in this chapter is in violation of the 1ˢᵗ Noahide Law.

(Mishnah Torah, Yesodi HaTorah 1:1-12)

1 The foundation of all foundations and the pillar of wisdom is to know that there is a Primary Being who brought into being all existence. All the beings of the heavens, the earth, and what is between them came into existence only from the truth of His being.

2 If one would imagine that He does not exist, no other being could possibly exist.

3 If one would imagine that none of the entities aside from Him exist, He alone would continue to exist, and the nullification of their [existence] would not nullify His existence, because all the [other] entities require Him and He, blessed be He, does not require them nor any one of them. Therefore, the truth of His [being] does not resemble the truth of any of their [beings].

4 This is implied by the prophet's statement [Jeremiah 10:10]: "And G-d, your L-rd, is true" - i.e., He alone is true and no other entity possesses truth that compares to His truth. This is what [is meant by] the Torah's statement [Deuteronomy 4:35]: "There is nothing else aside from Him" - i.e., aside from Him, there is no true existence like His.

5 This entity is the G-d of the world and the L-rd of the entire earth. He controls the sphere with infinite and unbounded power. This power [continues] without interruption, because the sphere is constantly revolving, and it is impossible for it to revolve without someone causing it to revolve. [That one is] He, blessed be He, who causes it to revolve without a hand or any [other] corporeal dimension.

6 The knowledge of this concept is a positive commandment, as [implied by Exodus 20:2]: "I am G-d, your L-rd...."

Anyone who presumes that there is another god transgresses a negative commandment, as [Exodus 20:3] states: "You shall have no other gods before Me" and denies a fundamental principle [of faith], because this is the great principle [of faith] upon which all depends.

7 This G-d is one. He is not two or more, but one, unified in a manner which [surpasses] any unity that is found in the world; i.e., He is not one in the manner of a general category which includes many individual entities, nor one in the way that the body is divided into different portions and dimensions. Rather, He is unified, and there exists no unity similar to His in this world.

If there were many gods, they would have body and form, because like entities are separated from each other only through the circumstances associated with body and form.

Were the Creator to have body and form, He would have limitation and definition, because it is impossible for a body not to be limited. And any entity which itself is limited and defined [possesses] only limited and defined power. Since our G-d, blessed be His name, possesses unlimited power, as evidenced by the continuous revolution of the sphere, we see that His power is not the power of a body. Since He is not a body, the circumstances associated with bodies that produce division and separation are not relevant to Him. Therefore, it is impossible for Him to be anything other than one.

The knowledge of this concept fulfills a positive commandment, as [implied by Deuteronomy 6:4]: "[Hear, Israel,] G-d is our L-rd, G-d is one."

8 Behold, it is explicitly stated in the Torah and [the works of] the prophets that the Holy One, blessed be He, is not [confined to] a body or physical form, as [Deuteronomy 4:39] states: "Because G-d, your L-rd, is the L-rd in the heavens above and the earth below," and a body cannot exist in two places [simultaneously].

Also, [Deuteronomy 4:15] states: "For you did not see any image," and [Isaiah 40:25] states: "To whom can you liken Me, with whom I will be equal." Were He [confined to] a body, He would resemble other bodies.

9 If so, what is the meaning of the expressions employed by the Torah: "Below His feet" [Exodus 24:10], "Written by the finger of G-d" [ibid. 31:18], "G-d's hand" [ibid. 9:3], "G-d's eyes" [Genesis 38:7], "G-d's ears" [Numbers 11:1], and the like?

All these [expressions were used] to relate to human thought processes which know only corporeal imagery, for the Torah speaks in the language of man. They are only descriptive terms, as [apparent from Deuteronomy 32:41]: "I will whet My lightning sword." Does He have a sword? Does He need a sword to kill? Rather, this is metaphoric imagery. [Similarly,] all [such expressions] are metaphoric imagery.

A proof of this concept: One prophet says that he saw the Holy One, blessed be He, "clothed in snow white" [Daniel 7:9], and another envisioned Him [coming] "with crimson garments from Batzra" [Isaiah 63:1]. Moses, our teacher, himself envisioned Him at the [Red] Sea as a mighty man, waging war, and, at Mount Sinai, [saw Him] as the leader of a congregation, wrapped [in a tallit].

This shows that He has no image or form. All these are merely expressions of prophetic vision and imagery and the truth of this concept cannot be grasped or comprehended by human thought. This is what the verse [Job 11:7] states: "Can you find the comprehension of G-d? Can you find the ultimate bounds of the Almighty?"

10 [If so,] what did Moses, our teacher, want to comprehend when he requested: "Please show me Your glory" [Exodus 33:18]?

He asked to know the truth of the existence of the Holy One, blessed be He, to the extent that it could be internalized within his mind, as one knows a particular person whose face he saw and whose image has been engraved within one's heart. Thus, this person's [identity] is distinguished within one's mind from [that of] other men. Similarly, Moses, our teacher, asked that the existence of the Holy One, blessed be He, be distinguished in his mind from the existence of other entities, to the extent that he would know the truth of His existence as it is [in its own right].

He, blessed be He, replied to him that it is not within the potential of a living man, [a creature of] body and soul, to comprehend this matter in its entirety. [Nevertheless,] He, blessed be He, revealed to [Moses] matters which no other man had known before him - nor would ever know afterward - until he was able to comprehend [enough] from the truth of His existence, for the Holy One, blessed be He, to be distinguished in his mind from other entities, as a person is distinguished from other men when one sees his back and knows the structure of his body and [the manner in which] he is clothed.

This is alluded to by the verse [Exodus 33:23]: "You shall see My back, but you shall not see My face."

11 Since it has been clarified that He does not have a body or corporeal form, it is also clear that none of the functions of the body are appropriate to Him: neither connection nor separation, neither place nor measure, neither ascent nor descent, neither right nor left, neither front nor back, neither standing nor sitting.

He is not found within time, so that He would possess a beginning, an end, or age. He does not change, for there is nothing that can cause Him to change.

[The concept of] death is not applicable to Him, nor is [that of] life within the context of physical life. [The concept of] foolishness is not applicable to Him, nor is [that of] wisdom in terms of human wisdom.

Neither sleep nor waking, neither anger nor laughter, neither joy nor sadness, neither silence nor speech in the human understanding of speech [are appropriate terms with which to describe Him]. Our Sages declared: "Above, there is no sitting or standing, separation or connection."

12 Since this is so, all such [descriptions] and the like which are related in the Torah and the words of the Prophets - all these are metaphors and imagery. *[For example,] "He who sits in the heavens shall laugh"* *[Psalms 2:4], "They angered Me with their emptiness" [Deuteronomy 32:21], and "As G-d rejoiced" [ibid. 28:63]. With regard to all such statements, our Sages said: "The Torah speaks in the language of man."*

This is [borne out by the rhetorical question (Jeremiah 7:19):] "Are they enraging Me?" Behold, [Malachi 3:6] states: "I, G-d, have not changed." Now were He to at times be enraged and at times be happy, He would change. Rather, all these matters are found only with regard to the dark and low bodies, those who dwell in houses of clay, whose foundation is dust. In contrast, He, blessed be He, is elevated and exalted above all this.

2) The prohibition against cursing G-d.

(Melachim uMilchamot 9:3)

A gentile who curses G-d's Name, whether he uses G-d's unique name or one of His other names, in any language, is liable. This law does not apply with regard to Jews.

(Melachim uMilchamot 2:6-9)

6 Whoever accepts a false god as true, even when he does not actually worship it, disgraces and blasphemes [G-d's] glorious and awesome name. This applies both to one who worships false gods and to one who curses G-d's name [as is obvious from Numbers 15:30]: "If a person commits [an act of idolatry] highhandedly, whether he be a native born [Jew] or a convert, he is blaspheming G-d."

Therefore, a person who worships false gods is to be hanged, just as one who blasphemes against G-d is hanged. Both are executed by being stoned to death. Therefore, I have included the laws applying to a blasphemer in Hilchot Avodat Kochavim. Both deny the fundamental principle [of Jewish faith].

7 These are the laws which govern a blasphemer: A blasphemer is not liable to be stoned to death until he states G-d's unique name, which possesses four letters: י-ב-ד-א, and curses that name with one of the names of G-d which are forbidden to be erased, as [Leviticus 24:16] states: "One who blasphemes G-d's name...."

One is obligated to be stoned to death for blaspheming G-d's unique name. [Should he blaspheme] the other names for G-d, he [transgresses] a prohibition.

There are those who state that one is liable [for execution] only when one blasphemes the name יה-ו-ה. I, however, maintain that one should be stoned to death in both instances.

8 Which verse serves as the warning prohibiting blasphemy? [Exodus 22:27]: "Do not curse G-d."

[The procedure for the trial of a blasphemer is as follows:] Each day [when] the witnesses are questioned, [they use] other terms for G-d's name, [stating,] "May Yosse strike Yosse." At the conclusion of the judgment, all bystanders are removed [from the courtroom]. The judges question the witness of greatest stature and tell him, "Tell us what you heard explicitly." He relates [the curse]. The judges stand upright and rend their garments. They may not mend them [afterwards].

The second witness states: "I also heard as he did." If there are many witnesses, they must all say, "I heard the same."

9 [The fact that] a blasphemer retracts his statements in the midst of speaking is of no consequence. Rather, once he utters blasphemy in the presence of witnesses, he is [liable for execution by] stoning.

Should a person curse G-d's name with the name of a false god, the zealous may strike him and slay him. If the zealous do not slay him and he is brought to court, he is not [condemned to] be stoned. [That punishment is administered] only when one curses G-d's name with another one of His unique names.

3) The prohibition against murder.

(Melachim uMilchamot 9:4)

A gentile who slays any soul, even a fetus in its mother's womb, should be executed in retribution for its death. Similarly, if he slew a person who would have otherwise died in the near future, placed a person before a lion, or starved a person to death, he should be executed for through one manner or other, he killed.

Similarly, one should be executed if he killed a pursuer when he could have saved the latter's potential victim by maiming one of the pursuer's limbs. These laws do not apply with regard to Jews.

4) The prohibition against incest and adultery.

(Melachim uMilchamot 9:5-8)

There are six illicit sexual relations forbidden to a gentile:
    a) his mother;
    b) his father's wife;
    c) a married woman;
    d) his maternal sister;
    e) a male;
    f) an animal.

These prohibitions are derived from the verse Genesis 2:24:
'Therefore, a man shall leave his father and his mother and cling to his wife and they shall become one flesh.'

'His father' - alludes to his father's wife;
'his mother' - is to be understood simply;
'cling to his wife' - and not his colleague's wife;
'his wife' - and not a male;
'They shall become one flesh' - this excludes a domesticated animal, beast, or fowl for man can never become 'one flesh' with them.

The prohibition against relations with a maternal sister is derived from the verse Genesis 20:13: 'She is my sister, my father's daughter, but not my mother's. Thus, she became my wife.'

A gentile is liable for relations with his mother even though she was seduced or raped by his father and never married to him. She is, nevertheless, his mother.

He is liable for relations with his father's wife even after his father's death.

He is liable for relations with a male whether a minor or an adult and with an animal whether young or old. In the latter instance, the gentile alone is executed and not the animal. We are only commanded to kill an animal with which a Jew engaged in relations.

A gentile is not executed for adultery with his colleague's wife unless they engage in relations in the normal manner after she had engaged in relations with her husband at least once. However, if she was merely consecrated or had undergone a wedding ceremony, but had never engaged in relations with her husband, one is not liable for engaging in relations with her, as Genesis 20:3 states: 'For she has been possessed by her husband.'

When does the above apply? When a gentile engages in relations with a gentile woman. However, a gentile who engages in relations with a married Jewess is liable whether their relations were carried out in a normal or abnormal manner.

Similarly, a gentile who engages in relations with a Jewish maiden who has been consecrated is stoned to death because of her as is the law regarding Jews. If he engages in relations with her after she has undergone the wedding ceremony, but has not engaged in relations with her husband, he is strangled to death as is the Jewish law. However, if he engages in relations with a Jewish woman after she engaged in relations with her husband once, he is sentenced to be executed by decapitation as if he had engaged in relations with a gentile woman.

A gentile who singles out one of his maid-servants for one of his slaves and, afterwards, engages in relations with her is executed because of her for violation of the prohibition against adultery. However, he is not liable for relations with her until the matter has become public knowledge and everyone refers to her as 'the wife of X, the slave.'

When do relations with her become permitted again? When he separates her from his slave and uncovers her hair in the market-place.

When is a gentile woman considered divorced? When her husband removes her from his home and sends her on her own or when she leaves his domain and goes her own way. They have no written divorce proceedings.

The matter is not dependent on the man's volition alone. Whenever he or she decide to separate, they may and then, are no longer considered as married.

5) The prohibition against theft.

(Melachim uMilchamot 9:9)

A gentile is liable for violating the prohibition against theft whether he stole from another gentile or from a Jew.

This applies to one who forcefully robs an individual or steals money, a kidnapper, an employer who withholds his worker's wages and the like, even a worker who eats from his employer's produce when he is not working. In all such cases, he is liable and is considered as a robber. With regard to Jews, the law is different.

Similarly, a gentile is liable for stealing an object worth less than a p'rutah [copper coin worth about a tenth of a loaf of bread]. Thus, if one gentile stole an object worth less than a p'rutah and another gentile stole it from him, they are both executed because of it.

6) The command to establish laws and courts of justice.

(Melachim uMilchamot 9:14)

How must the gentiles fulfill the commandment to establish laws and courts? They are obligated to set up judges and magistrates in every major city to render judgement concerning these six mitzvot and to admonish the people regarding their observance.

A gentile who transgresses these seven commands shall be executed by decapitation. For this reason, all the inhabitants of Shechem were obligated to die. Shechem kidnapped. They observed and were aware of his deeds, but did not judge him.

A gentile is executed on the basis of the testimony of one witness and the verdict of a single judge. No warning is required. Relatives may serve as witnesses. However, a woman may not serve as a witness or a judge for them.

7) The prohibition against eating flesh with its lifeblood.

(Melachim uMilchamot 9:10-13)

Similarly, a gentile is liable for violating the prohibition against eating a limb or flesh from a living creature. This applies regardless of the amount involved, for the specification of minimum amounts only applies to Jews.

A gentile is permitted blood from a living creature.

The prohibition applies to a limb or flesh that is separated from either a domesticated animal or a beast. However, it appears to me that a gentile is not executed for eating a limb taken from a living bird.

Though one slaughters an animal, even if one severs the two signs that distinguish it as having been slaughtered in a kosher manner, as long as the animal moves convulsively, the limbs and meat which are separated from it are forbidden to a gentile because of the prohibition against a limb from a living creature.

All prohibitions that apply to a Jew regarding a limb from a living creature also apply to gentiles. Furthermore, there are instances where a gentile would be held liable and a Jew will not for a gentile is liable for a limb or flesh from a living creature whether from a domesticated animal or a beast, whether from a kosher or non-kosher species.

Similarly, a gentile is forbidden to partake of a limb from a living creature for a limb or flesh which is separated from an animal that is moving convulsively even though a Jew has already severed the two signs.

This may be a lot to take in at first, but understand that learning is a lifelong pursuit. This is merely an overview of the Seven Laws for the purpose of providing a kosher introduction to these subjects. Every person should pursue a lifetime of learning and good deeds on the righteous path.

"These are the matters that have no measure: the corner [of the field for the poor], the first fruits offering, pilgrimage [to the Temple], acts of kindness, and Torah Study" (Mishnah, Pe'ah 1:1).

These five matters are not given measure because each should do according to his ability. As we mature, these measures increase. As these measures increase, we mature.

TRUE or FALSE

1. The first six of the seven Noahide Laws were given to Adam.

2. Law One is the prohibition against worship of false gods.

3. Law Two is the prohibition against cursing G-d.

4. Law Three is the prohibition against murder.

5. Law Four is the prohibition against incest and adultery.

6. Law Five is the prohibition against theft.

7. Law Six is the command to establish laws and courts of justice.

8. Law Seven is the prohibition against eating flesh from a living animal.

9. Each of the seven should be practiced by all people as prescribed by *halachah* (Jewish Law).

10. Redefining the Noahide laws according to your own intellect and understanding is creating your own *mitzvah* and religion.

11. It is NOT important for a person to acknowledge the validity and preservation of the Oral Torah in order to perform the Noahide laws in the proper manner and be a righteous gentile.

12. G-d is not dependent on anything to exist, and without G-d nothing would exist.

13. The truth of G-d's being does not resemble the truth of any other thing that exists.

14. G-d is completely one, with no divisions, nor many individual entities, nor parts like a body, nor dimensions, unlike any other unity in this world.

15. G-d is not limited; therefore, he has not body or form.

16. Human imagery of G-d is used metaphorically to express concepts to us in a way we can understand as human beings, but does not mean that G-d has any physicality or corporeality.

17. G-d does not change, so he can't be born, die, ascend, descend, sleep, wake, laugh, become angry, become sad, speak, become silent. All mentions of such changes are metaphoric in nature.

18. G-d is above all things of this world and all intellectual ideas.

19. It is not permissible for a gentile to slay a fetus in the mother's womb.

20. The six illicit sexual relations prohibited to a gentile are his mother, his father's wife, a married woman, his maternal sister, a male, and an animal.

21. Some examples of theft are kidnapping, an employer withholding wages, and an employee eating from his employer's produce while he isn't working.

22. A gentile who transgresses the Seven is obligated to die.

23. The flesh of a living animal is a limb that is moving convulsively, even when the animal has been slaughtered in a kosher manner.

ANSWERS

All answers are TRUE.

IDOLATRY

THIS CHAPTER ELABORATES on the prohibition against worship of false gods and the prohibition against cursing G-d. The previous chapter gives an introduction to understanding these laws. This chapter elaborates on the subject of properly identifying false gods, blasphemy, false prophets, and false worship.

Rambam identifies 51 mitzvot pertaining to this topic in Hilchos Avodat Kochavim in Mishnah Torah.

1. Not to show interest in the worship of false gods

2. Not to stray after the thoughts of one's heart or the sights one's eyes behold

3. Not to curse [G-d]

4. Not to worship [false gods] with the types of service with which they are customarily served

5. Not to bow down to [false gods]

6. Not to make an idol for oneself

7. Not to make an idol even for others

8. *Not to make images even for decoration*
9. *Not to persuade others to [worship false gods]*
10. *To burn an apostate city*
11. *Never to rebuild it*
12. *Not to derive benefit from any of its property*
13. *Not to persuade a single individual to worship [false gods]*
14. *Not to love a mesit*
15. *Not to reduce one's hatred for him*
16. *Not to save his life*
17. *Not to advance any arguments on his behalf*
18. *Not to withhold information that will lead to his conviction*
19. *Not to prophesy in the name of [false gods]*
20. *Not to listen to anyone who prophesies in the name of [false gods]*
21. *Not to give false prophecy even in the name of G-d*
22. *Not to fear executing a false prophet*
23. *Not to swear in the name of a false god*
24. *Not to perform the deeds associated with an ov*
25. *Not to perform the deeds associated with a yid'oni*
26. *Not to offer to Molech*
27. *Not to erect a pillar [for purposes of worship]*
28. *Not to prostrate oneself on hewn stones*
29. *Not to plant an asherah*
30. *To destroy false gods and all their objects of worship*
31. *Not to benefit from false gods and all their objects of worship*
32. *Not to benefit from ornaments that have adorned false gods*
33. *Not to establish a covenant with nations who worship false gods*
34. *Not to show them favor*
35. *Not to allow them to settle in our land*
36. *Not to follow their customs or manner of dress*
37. *Not to act as a soothsayer*
38. *Not to practice black magic*
39. *Not to practice divination*
40. *Not to cast spells*
41. *Not to seek information from the dead*
42. *Not to consult an ov*
43. *Not to consult a yid'oni*
44. *Not to practice sorcery;*
45. *Not to shave the temples of our heads*

46. Not to shave off the corners of our beards

47. For a man not to wear a woman's apparel

48. For a woman not to wear armament or a man's apparel

49. Not to tattoo [one's body]

50. Not to make cuts in one's flesh

51. Not to tear out hair [in mourning] for the dead

From the understanding of these 51 *mitzvot*, we gain insight into what are inappropriate methods of worshipping G-d, what is considered worship of false gods, and how to identify false prophets.

False g-ds.

(Mishnah Torah, Avodat Kochavim 2:1-5)

1 The essence of the commandment [forbidding] the worship of false gods is not to serve any of the creations, not an angel, a sphere, or a star, none of the four fundamental elements, nor any entity created from them. Even if the person worshiping knows that 'ה is the [true] G-d and serves the creation in the manner in which Enosh and the people of his generation worshiped [the stars] originally, he is considered to be an idol worshiper.

The Torah warns us about this, saying [Deuteronomy 4:19]: "Lest you lift your eyes heavenward and see the sun, the moon, and the stars... [and bow down and worship them], the entities which G-d apportioned to all the nations." This implies that you might inquire with "the eye of the heart" and it might appear to you that these entities control the world, having been apportioned by G-d to all the nations to be alive, to exist, and not to cease existence, as is the pattern of [the other creations with] the world. Therefore, you might say that it is worthy to bow down to them and worship them.

For this reason, [Deuteronomy 11:16] commands: "Be very careful that your heart not be tempted [to go astray and worship other gods]." This implies that the thoughts of your heart should not lead you astray to worship these and make them an intermediary between you and the Creator.

2 The worshipers of false gods have composed many texts concerning their service, [describing] what is the essence of their service, what practices are involved, and what are its statutes. The Holy One, blessed be He, has commanded us not to read those books at all, nor to think about them or any matters involved with them.

It is even forbidden to look at the image of an idol, as [Leviticus 19:4] states: "Do not turn to the idols." In this regard, [Deuteronomy 12:30] states: "[Be careful]... lest you seek to find out about their gods, saying, 'How did they serve them.' This prohibits inquiring about the nature of their service even if you, yourself, do not serve them. This matter will ultimately cause you to turn to [the false god] and worship it as they do, as [the above verse continues]: "so that I will do the same."

3 All these prohibitions have one common thrust: that one should not pay attention to idol worship. Whoever performs a deed that reflects his concern with [idol worship] receives lashes [as punishment].

The worship of false gods is not the only subject to which we are forbidden to pay attention; rather, we are warned not to consider any thought which will cause us to uproot one of the fundamentals of the Torah. We should not turn our minds to these matters, think about them, or be drawn after the thoughts of our hearts.

In general, people have limited powers of understanding, and not all minds are capable of appreciating the truth in its fullness. [Accordingly,] were a person to follow the thoughts of his heart, it is possible that he would destroy the world because of his limited understanding.

What is implied? There are times when a person will stray after star worship, and times when he will wonder about G-d's oneness: Perhaps He is one, perhaps He is not? [He might also wonder:] What exists above, [in the heavenly realms]? What exists below [them]? What was before time? What will be after time? Similarly, [one might wonder about] prophecy: Perhaps it is true, perhaps it is not? And [one may also wonder] about the Torah: Perhaps it emanates from G-d, perhaps it does not?

Since he may not know the guidelines with which to evaluate [ideas that will lead him] to the truth in its fullness, he may come to heresy. The Torah has warned about this matter, saying [Numbers 15:39]: "Do not stray after your hearts and eyes, which have led you to immorality" - i.e., each one of you should not follow his limited powers of understanding and think that he has comprehended the truth.

Our Sages [interpreted this warning]: "After your hearts," this refers to heresy; "after your eyes," this refers to immorality. This prohibition - though [severe,] causing a person to be prevented [from attaining a portion] in the world to come - is not punishable by lashes.

4 The commandment [forbidding] the worship of false gods is equivalent to all the mitzvot, as [implied by Numbers 15:22]: "Lest you err and not perform all the mitzvot...." The oral tradition teaches that the verse refers to the worship of false gods. Thus, we learn that anyone who acknowledges a false god denies the entire Torah in its totality, all the works of the prophets, and everything that has been commanded to the prophets from Adam, [the first man,] until eternity, as [Numbers 15:23] continues: "...from the day G-d issued His commandments and afterwards, for your future generations."

[Conversely,] anyone who denies the worship of false gods acknowledges the entire Torah in its totality, all the works of the prophets, and everything that has been commanded to the prophets from Adam, [the first man,] until eternity. [This acknowledgement] is fundamental to all of the mitzvot.

5 A Jew who serves false gods is considered like a gentile in all regards and is not comparable to a Jew who violated another transgression punishable by being stoned to death. An apostate who worships false gods is considered to be an apostate with regard to the entire Torah.

Similarly, Jewish minnim are not considered to be Jews with regard to any matter. Their repentance should never be accepted, as [implied by Proverbs 2:19]: "None that go to her repent, nor will they regain the paths of life."

The minnim are those who stray after the thoughts of their hearts, concerning themselves with the foolish matters mentioned above, until they ultimately transgress against the body of Torah [law] arrogantly, with scorn, with the intent of provoking G-d's anger, and yet say that there is no sin involved.

It is forbidden to talk to them or to reply to them at all, as [Proverbs 5:8] states: "Do not come close to her door." [It can be assumed that] a min's thoughts are concerned with false gods.

Idol worship.

(Mishnah Torah, Avodat Kochavim 3)

1 Whoever serves false gods willingly, as a conscious act of defiance, is liable for kerat [cut off]. If witnesses who warned him were present, he is [punished by being] stoned to death. If he served [such gods] inadvertently, he must bring a fixed sin offering.

2 The gentiles established various different services for each particular idol and image. These services do not [necessarily] resemble each other. For example, Pe'or is served by defecating before it. Marculis is served by throwing stones at it or clearing stones away from it. Similarly, other services were instituted for other idols.

One who defecates before Marculis or throws a stone at Pe'or is free of liability until he serves it according to the accepted modes of service, as [implied by Deuteronomy 12:30]: "[Lest one inquire about their gods, saying,] 'How did these nations serve their gods? I will do the same.'"

For this reason, a court must know the types of worship [practiced by gentiles], because an idolater is stoned to death only when we know that [he has worshiped a false god] in the mode in which it is traditionally worshiped.

3 The warning [forbidding] such worship and the like is the verse [Exodus 20:5] which states: "Do not serve them."

When does the above apply? with regard to services other than bowing, slaughtering [an animal], bringing a burnt offering, and offering a libation. A person who performs one of these four services to any one of the types of false gods is liable, even though this is not its accepted mode of service.

How is this exemplified? A person who offers a libation to Pe'or or slaughters [an animal] to Marculis is liable, as [implied by Exodus 22:19]: "Whoever slaughters [an animal] to any deity other than G-d alone must be condemned to death."

[Liability for performing the other services can be derived as follows:] Slaughter was included in the general category of services [forbidden to be performed to false gods]. Why was it mentioned explicitly? To teach [the following]: Slaughter is distinct as one of the services of G-d, and one who slaughters to false gods is liable to be executed by stoning. Similarly, with regard to any service which is distinct as one of the services of G-d, if a person performs it in worship of other gods, he is liable.

For [a similar reason, Exodus 34:14] states: "Do not bow down to another god," to teach that one is liable for bowing down [to another god] even when this is not its accepted mode of service. The same applies to one who brings a burnt offering or pours a libation. Sprinkling [blood] is considered the same as pouring a libation.

4 [Even if] one pours feces before it or pours a libation of urine from a chamber pot before it, one is liable. If one slaughters a locust before it, one is not liable, unless this is the mode of service of that deity. Similarly, if one slaughters an animal lacking a limb for it, one is not liable, unless this is the manner of service of this deity.

[The following rules apply when] a false god is worshiped by [beating with] a staff [before it]: If one breaks a staff before it, one is liable [for the worship of false gods], and [the deity] is forbidden. If one threw a staff before it, one is held liable, but [the deity] is not forbidden, because throwing a staff is not considered equivalent to sprinkling blood. The staff remains as it was, while the blood spatters [in different directions].

A person who accepts any one of the various false gods as a deity is liable for [execution by] stoning. Even one who lifted up a brick and said, "You are my god," or the like, is liable. Even if he retracted his statements in the midst of speaking and said, "This is not my G-d," his retraction is not significant and he should be stoned [to death].

5 Anyone who serves a false god through its accepted mode of service - even if he does so in a derisive manner - is liable. What is implied? When a person defecates before Pe'or to repudiate it, or throws a stone at Marculis to repudiate it - since this is the manner of serving them - the person is liable and must bring a sacrifice [to atone for] his inadvertent transgression.

6 [The following rules apply when] a person serves a false deity out of love - i.e., he desires an image because its service is very attractive - or when one serves it out of his fear of it - i.e., he fears that it will harm him - as the [idol] worshipers fear [their deities as sources of] benefit and harm: If he accepts it as a god, he is liable to be stoned to death. If he serves it out of love or fear through its accepted mode of service or through one of the four services [mentioned above], he is not held liable.

One who embraces a false deity, kisses it, sweeps before it, mops before it, washes it, anoints it, dresses it, places shoes upon it, or performs any similar act of deference violates a negative commandment, as [implied by Exodus 20:5]: "Do not serve them." Such acts are also "service." The offender is, nevertheless, not liable for lashes, because [these services] are not [mentioned] explicitly [by the Torah].

If one of the above services was the accepted mode of worship [of a particular deity] and a person performed this service as an act of worship, he is liable [for execution].

7 If a splinter becomes stuck in a person's foot before an idol, he should not bend down to remove it, because it appears that he is bowing down to the idol.

If money belonging to a person becomes scattered before an idol, he should not bow down and pick it up, because it appears that he is bowing down to the idol. Instead, he should sit down, and then pick it up.

8 A person should not place his mouth over the mouths of statues which serve as fountains that are located before false deities in order to drink, because it appears that he is kissing the false deity.

9 A person who has a false god made for himself - even though he, himself, did not actually fashion it, nor worship it - is [punished by] lashing, as [Exodus 20:5] states: "Do not make for yourself an idol or any representation."

Similarly, a person who actually fashions a false god for others, even for idolaters, is [punished by] lashing, as [Leviticus 19:4] states: "Do not make molten gods for yourselves." Accordingly, a person who actually fashions a false god1for himself receives two measures of lashes.

10 It is prohibited to make images for decorative purposes, even though they do not represent false deities, as [implied by Exodus 20:23]: "Do not make with Me [gods of silver and gods of gold]." This refers even to images of gold and silver which are intended only for decorative purposes, lest others err and view them as deities.

It is forbidden to make decorative images of the human form alone. Therefore, it is forbidden to make human images with wood, cement, or stone. This [prohibition] applies when the image is protruding - for example, images and sculptures made in a hallway and the like. A person who makes such an image is [liable for] lashes.

In contrast, it is permitted to make human images that are engraved or painted - e.g., portraits, whether on wood or on stone - or that are part of a tapestry.

11 [The following rules apply regarding] a signet ring which bears a human image: If the image is protruding, it is forbidden to wear it, but it is permitted to use it as a seal. If the image is an impression, it is permitted to wear it, but it is forbidden to use it as a seal, because it will create an image which protrudes.

Similarly, it is forbidden to make an image of the sun, the moon, the stars, the constellations, or the angels, as [implied by Exodus, ibid.]: "Do not make with Me [gods of silver...]" - i.e., do not make images of My servants, those who serve before Me on high. This [prohibition] applies even [to pictures] on tablets.

The images of animals and other living beings - with the exception of men - and similarly, the images of trees, grasses, and the like may be fashioned. This applies even to images which protrude.

(Mishnah Torah, Avodat Kochavim 6:6)

A monument which the Torah has forbidden is a structure around which people gather. [This prohibition applies] even [when it was constructed] for the service of G-d, because this is a pagan practice, as [Deuteronomy 16:22] states: "Do not erect a monument which G-d hates." Whoever erects a monument is [liable for] lashes.

(Mishnah Torah, Avodat Kochavim 7:1-3)

1 It is a positive commandment to destroy false deities, all their accessories, and everything that is made for their purposes, as [Deuteronomy 12:2] states: "You shall surely destroy all the places [where the gentiles... served their gods]" and, as [implied by Deuteronomy 7:5]: "Rather, what you should do to them is tear down their altars."

In Eretz Yisrael, the mitzvah requires us to hunt after idol worship until it is eradicated from our entire land. In the diaspora, however, we are not required to hunt after it. Rather, whenever we conquer a place, we must destroy all the false deities contained within.

[The source for this distinction is Deuteronomy 12:3, which] states: "And you shall destroy their name from this place," [implying that] you are obligated to hunt false deities in Eretz Yisrael, but you are not obligated to do so in the diaspora.

2 It is forbidden to benefit from false deities, their accessories, offerings for them, and anything made for them, as [implied by Deuteronomy 7:26]: "Do not bring an abomination to your home."

Anyone who derives benefit from any of the above receives two measures of lashes: one because of the prohibition, "Do not bring an abomination...," and one because of the prohibition, "Let nothing which is condemned cling to your hand."

3 It is forbidden to benefit from an animal which was sacrificed to false deities in its entirety - even its excrement, its bones, its horns, its hooves, and its hide. It is forbidden to benefit from it at all.

To cite an example, the hide of an animal which is marked by a sign that indicates that it was offered as a sacrifice to false deities - e.g., it has a round hole in the place of the heart through which the heart is extracted, which was a common practice [of idolaters] - It is forbidden to benefit from all of these hides and others of the like.

(Mishnah Torah, Avodat Kochavim 8:6)

How must one destroy a false deity and the other entities which are forbidden on its account - e.g., its accessories and offerings? One must grind them and scatter [the dust] in the wind, or burn them and deposit the ashes in the Dead Sea.

Dealings with idolaters.

(Mishnah Torah, Avodat Kochavim 9:1-5)

1 It is forbidden to purchase or sell any durable entity to an idolater within three days of one of their holidays. [Similarly, within this period, it is forbidden] to borrow from them, to lend to them, to accept payment from them or to repay them for a loan that is supported by a promissory note or collateral. It is, however, permitted to collect a loan which is supported by a verbal commitment alone, because one is saving one's property from being lost to them.

It is permitted to sell them an entity which will not endure - e.g., vegetables, or a cooked dish - until the day of their festival.

When does the above apply? In Eretz Yisrael. In other lands, however, it is forbidden [to engage in such activities] only on the day of their festival itself.

If one transgressed and did business with them during these three days, one may derive benefit from the results of these transactions. When, however, one does business with them on the day of their festival itself, it is forbidden to benefit from the results of these transactions.

2 It is forbidden to send a present to a gentile on one of his holidays, unless one knows that he does not acknowledge or worship idols. Similarly, if a gentile sends a present to a Jew on one of [the gentile's] holidays, the Jew should not accept it. If, however, there is the possibility of ill-feeling arising, he should take it from him. Nevertheless, he should not derive any benefit from it until he finds out that the gentile does not acknowledge or worship idols.

3 If the idolaters' festival lasts several days - whether three, four, or ten - all the days [of the festival] are considered as a single day. [Carrying out transactions] on any of these days, or on the three days preceding them, is forbidden.

4 The Canaanites are idol worshipers, and Sunday is their festival. Accordingly, in Eretz Yisrael, it is forbidden to conduct transactions with them on Thursday and Friday each and every week, and, needless to say, on Sunday itself, when transactions with them are forbidden everywhere.

5 The day on which the idolaters gather together to crown a king and offer sacrifice and praise to their false deities is considered to be one of their holidays, since it is comparable to their other holidays. In contrast, on a day which is celebrated by an individual idolater as a festival on which he gives thanks and praise to the star he [worships] - for example, his birthday, the day on which he shaves his beard or hair, the day on which he returns from a sea-voyage, the day on which he leaves prison, the day on which he makes a [wedding] feast for his son, and the like - it is forbidden [to do business] on that particular day only with that individual man.

Similarly, when [it is customary] that the day on which one of them dies is marked with festivities, it is forbidden [to do business] with those individuals on that day. Whenever [a person's] death is marked by the burning of his utensils and the offering of incense, we can assume that idol worship is [involved in the ritual].

The [above] prohibition applies only to those who worship [the false deity]. In contrast, it is permitted to do business with those who join in the celebrations by eating, drinking, and observing it as a matter of custom or in deference to the king.

False evangelists & false prophets.

(Mishnah Torah, Avodat Kochavim 3)

1 A person who proselytizes [a mesit] to any single Jew [a musat] - whether man or woman - on behalf of false deities should be stoned to death. [This applies] even if neither the mesit or the musat actually worshiped the false deity.

As long as he instructed him to worship [the false deity], he should be executed by stoning, regardless of whether the mesit was a prophet or an ordinary person, or whether the musat was a single individual - man or woman - or whether several people were proselytized.

2 A person who proselytizes the majority of the inhabitants of a city is called a madiach rather than a mesit. If the person who leads the majority of a city astray is a prophet, he is executed by stoning, and the people who were led astray are judged as individuals, and are not considered to be inhabitants of an ir hanidachas[wayward city] [For the latter laws to be applied,] two people must proselytize them.

If a person says: "A false deity told me: 'Serve me,'" or "The Holy One, blessed be He, told me: 'Serve a false deity'" - he is considered a prophet who leads others astray. If the majority of the city's inhabitants are swayed by his words, he should be stoned to death.

A mesit should be stoned to death whether he proselytizes in plural terms or in singular. What is implied? He is considered a mesit if he tells a colleague, "I will worship a false deity. [Follow me.] I will go and worship..." or "Let us go and worship following the particular rite with which that deity is served," "I will slaughter. [Follow me.] I will go and slaughter..." or "Let us go and slaughter," "I will bring a burnt offering. [Follow me.] I will go and bring a burnt offering..." or "Let us go and bring a burnt offering," "I will offer a libation. [Follow me.] I will go and offer a libation..." or "Let us go and offer a libation," or "I will bow down. [Follow me.] I will go and bow down..." or "Let us go and bow down."

When a person proselytizes two individuals, they may serve as witnesses against him. They should summon him to court and testify against him, relating what he told them, and the mesit is stoned.

3 A mesit does not need a warning.

If one proselytizes a single individual, the latter should tell him, "I have friends who would also be interested in this," and thus he should lure him into proselytizing before two people, so that the mesit can be executed.

If the mesit refuses to proselytize before two people, it is a mitzvah to set a trap for him. A trap is never set for a person who violates any of the Torah's other prohibitions. This is the only exception.

How is the trap set for him? The musat should bring two people and place them in a dark place where they can see the mesit and hear what he is saying without his seeing them. He tells the mesit: "Repeat what you told me privately."

[When] he does so, the musat should reply: "How can we forsake our G-d in heaven and serve wood and stone?" If [the mesit] retracts or remains silent, he is not held liable. If he tells him, "This is our obligation and this is beneficial to us," those who stand far off have him summoned to court and stoned.

4 It is a mitzvah for the musat to kill [the mesit], as [Deuteronomy 13:10] states: "Your hand must be the first against him to kill him."

It is forbidden for the musat to love the mesit, as [the previous verse states]: "Do not be attracted to him." Since [Exodus 23:5] states with regard to an enemy: "You must surely help him," [the question arises:] Perhaps you should help a mesit? The Torah [Deuteronomy, ibid.] teaches, "Do not... listen to him."

Since [Leviticus 19:16] teaches: "Do not stand idly over your brother's blood," [the question arises:] Perhaps you should not stand idly over a mesit's blood? The Torah teaches, [Deuteronomy, ibid.] "Do not let your eyes pity him."

The musat is forbidden to advance any arguments on his behalf, as [the verse continues,] "Do not show him any compassion." If he knows incriminating evidence, he is not permitted to remain silent, as [the verse continues,] "Do not try to cover up for him."

What is the verse which serves as a warning against a common person proselytizing as a mesit? "And all Israel will hear and they will become afraid [and they will not continue to do such evil things]" (Deuteronomy 13:12).

5 [The following rules apply to] a person who proselytizes others by telling them to worship him: Should he tell them: "Worship me," and they worship him, he should be stoned. If they did not worship him, even though they accepted and agreed to his statements, he is not liable for stoning.

In contrast, if he proselytizes by telling them to worship another man or another false deity, [different rules apply:] If they accept his statements and say, "We will go and worship," even if they have not actually worshiped, both of them - the mesit and the musat - should be stoned. [Deuteronomy 13:9] states: "Do not be attracted to him or listen to him." Thus, if one was attracted and listened, one is held liable.

6 What is meant by [the expression,] a prophet who prophesies in the name of false gods? A person who says: "This false deity or this star told me that we are commanded to do such and such or to refrain from doing so." [This applies] even when he stated the law accurately, labeling the impure as impure and the pure as pure.

If a warning was given to him [beforehand], he is executed by strangulation, as [Deuteronomy 18:20] states: "And one who speaks in the name of other gods, that prophet shall die." The warning against this [transgression] is included in the statement, [Exodus 23:13:] "And you shall not mention the name of other gods."

7 It is forbidden to enter into a discussion or a debate with one who prophesies in the name of a false deity. We may not ask him to perform a sign or wonder, and if he does so on his own accord, we should pay no attention to it nor think about it. Whoever contemplates about the wonders [he performed, thinking], "Perhaps they are true," violates a negative commandment, as [Deuteronomy 13:4] states: "Do not listen to the words of that prophet."

Similarly, a false prophet should be executed by strangulation. [He is to be executed] although he speaks in the name of G-d and neither adds to nor diminishes [the mitzvot], as [Deuteronomy 18:20] states: "However, the prophet who dares to speak a matter in My name which I did not command - that prophet shall die."

8 [The category of] a false prophet includes:
a) one who "prophesies" regarding something that was never heard through prophetic vision;
b) one who "prophesies" about a subject which he heard from another prophet, saying that this prophecy was given to him.

[Both of these individuals] are to be executed by strangulation.

9 Anyone who refrains from executing a false prophet because of the latter's [spiritual] level, [as expressed by] his adherence to the paths of prophecy, violates a negative commandment, as [Deuteronomy 18:22] states: "Do not fear him." Similarly, included within [the scope of the prohibition:] "Do not fear him" are one who withholds incriminating testimony against [a false prophet] and one who is afraid or in awe of his words.

A false prophet may be tried only by the [supreme] court of 71 judges.

10 A person who makes a vow or takes an oath in the name of a false deity is [liable for] lashes, as [Exodus 23:13] states: "And you shall not mention the name of other gods."

[This applies] both to one who takes such an oath for his own reasons and to one who takes such an oath because of a gentile. It is forbidden to have a gentile take an oath on his deity. It is even forbidden to mention the name of a gentile deity without any connection to an oath, as [implied by the expression], "You shall not mention."

11 A person should not tell a colleague: "Wait for me near a particular false deity," or the like.

It is permitted to mention the name of any false deity that is mentioned in the Bible - e.g., Peor, Ba'al, Nevo, Gad, and the like. It is forbidden to cause others to take oaths or vows in the name of false deities. [In regard to all these prohibitions,] the only [transgressor] liable for lashes is one who [himself] makes a vow or an oath in the name [of a false deity].

Hillel & The Floating Skull

One day as Hillel was walking along the river, he noticed a skull floating on the water. He turned to the skull and said, "You were drowned because you drowned others. And ultimately those who drowned you will also drown."

Over 1,000 years later, Rambam commented on the story saying that there are consequences to our actions that reflect the actions themselves. You will receive punishment in the form of your crime. If you invent an unjust thing to benefit yourself at the expense of others, that unjust thing will ultimately be used against you. The same goes for positive actions. If you introduce something that benefits others, that thing will ultimately benefit you.

This is called "measure for measure."

Because of Hillel's humility and length of his life (120 years) among other reasons, the mystical tradition is that Moses and Hillel shared the same soul. Rambam's grandson, Rabbi David Hanagid, cites a tradition passed down by "the early ones" that the skull actually belonged to Pharaoh.

So, we have the Moses and Pharaoh story being revisited in Hillel's lifetime. He was telling Pharaoh "Because you commanded that the Jewish children be drowned in the Nile, you were drowned."

When Hillel came across Pharaoh's skull, he thought to himself, "Why has G-d arranged for me to see this sight?" He then came to the conclusion that the time had finally come for Pharaoh's soul to find peace.

By using Pharaoh as an example to teach something meaningful, Hillel uplifted Pharaoh's soul and granted it the ability to find peace.

This mystical story is very fitting as a conclusion to this chapter. In a world where we are surrounded by idolatry, it is not uncommon to be provoked to thinking it is our duty to drown the armies of evangelists and false prophets that are following "god-men" like Pharaoh.

This is not proper behavior.

The eleventh of the Thirteen Principles of Faith is "The belief in divine reward and retribution." There is no power outside of HaShem, and He will bring all things into account "measure for measure," just as He did with Pharaoh.

Rather than being one who drowns others, we should be humble like Hillel, observing the world around us and bringing souls to peace with the knowledge of Torah. As Hillel often said, "love peace and pursue peace, love all G-d's creations and bring them close to the Torah."

TRUE or FALSE

1. Rambam identifies 51 mitzvot pertaining to this topic in Hilchos Avodat Kochavim in Mishnah Torah.

2. It is prohibited to show interest in the worship of false gods.

3. It is prohibited to make images even for decoration.

4. It is prohibited to love a mesit, one who persuades a single individual to worship false gods.

5. It is prohibited to listen to anyone who prophesies in the name of false gods.

6. It is prohibited to prostrate oneself on hewn stones.

7. It is prohibited to benefit from false gods and all their objects of worship.

8. It is prohibited to allow people who worship false gods to settle in the land of Israel.

9. It is prohibited to seek information from the dead.

10. It is prohibited for a man to wear women's apparel and for a woman to wear a man's apparel.

11. It is prohibited to tattoo one's body.

12. It is prohibited to make cuts in one's flesh.

13. It is prohibited to tear out hair in mourning for the dead.

ANSWERS

All answers are TRUE.

MASHIACH

THIS CHAPTER ON *MASHIACH* was not included in the original outline of this book because discussing the subject of *Mashiach* can often be a challenging concept. Not everyone on their journey is ready to hear what Judaism teaches about *Mashiach*.

It must be known that the intention of this chapter is not to insult or attack other religions, deities, or prophets. Nor is it meant to be an apologetic for Judaism. Rather, this chapter is constructed in the same format as the rest of the book, which is to give a simple straight forward explanation of what Judaism teaches on foundational Jewish concepts.

Whereas other chapters may be delicious to one seeking kosher Torah but dull to others, this chapter has the potential to be the most emotionally stirring chapter for everyone who has ever had any kind of relationship to Christianity or Christian doctrines.

Therefore, if anyone takes this knowledge and uses it as a way to harm his neighbor is operating outside of the intent of this book. Please do not misuse this information.

Let's bring this into perspective before we get into the subject of *Mashiach.*

Imagine if you were going to be tormented by incredible pain for an infinite amount of time because you made a bad decision. However, a person travels an incalculable distance and struggles an incalculable amount to substitute himself for you.

The average Christian (which includes the Christ-following sects of Messianics and Hebrew Roots) really believes that G-d became a man and suffered for you, and if you believe in him, you will be saved. Not only that, but many Christians are genuinely caring and loving people, and they believe this to the core of their being. Christians are in love with this man and talk to him all the time, resting their deepest most intimate shortcomings and joys upon him.

Imagine telling this person that this very stirring and ultimate depiction of the one they have deeply loved all of their life is not accurate. It's like telling someone their spouse isn't real, or their marriage is fake.

Wouldn't this be highly offensive to any person?

As stated previously, it should be well known that this chapter is not intended to hurt or offend other religions. Rather, it is to share a basic understanding of what Judaism teaches about *Mashiach.*

Without further ado, let's begin.

What is a *Mashiach*?

Mashiach comes from the root word *mashach,* which means "to anoint" with oil by pouring over the top. Therefore, a *mashiach* is one who has been "anointed" by oil being poured over his head.

There are two offices that are *mashach,* making two different kinds of *mashiach,* the *Kohen HaMashiach* (Anointed Priest) and *Melech HaMashiach* (Anointed King).

Mashiach appears 39 times in 38 verses in the *Tenakh.* Each of the four times the word *mashiach* appears in the Torah, it is in reference to the *Kohen HaMashiach,* the "Anointed Priest" (Lev 4:3,5,16; 6:22).

The first *Kohen HaMashiach* was Aaron, the brother of Moses.

And [Moses] poured some of the anointing oil on Aaron's head and anointed [mashach] him to consecrate him. (Leviticus 8:12)

Behold, how good and pleasant it is when brothers dwell in unity! It is like the precious oil on the head, running down on the beard, on the beard of Aaron, running down on the collar of his robes! (Psalm 133:1-2)

The first *Melech HaMashiach* (Anointed King) was King Saul.

Samuel took a flask of oil and poured some on [Saul's] head and kissed him, and said, "HaShem herewith anoints [mashach] you ruler over His own people." (1Samuel 10:1)

It is important to note that it is forbidden for one man to be both the King and High Priest, let alone that it is physically impossible. The *Kohen HaMashiach* must come from the lineage of Aaron, descendant of Levi. The *Melech HaMashiach* must come from the lineage of

Solomon, descendant of Judah. Levi and Judah were brothers. Since lineage is established through paternity, one is either a son of Judah or a son of Levi, but can't be a son of both tribes.

When we discuss "The" *Mashiach,* we are referring to the future *Melech HaMashiach* (Anointed King) of Israel from the line of King David through Solomon, excluding the lineage of Jechoniah. Jechoniah was the king of Judah that surrendered the nation of Israel into the Babylonian captivity to King Nebukadnetstsar.

> *Is this man Jechoniah a despised, broken pot, a vessel no one cares for? Why are he and his children hurled and cast into a land that they do not know?*
> *O land, land, land, hear the word of HaShem!*
> *Thus says HaShem: "Write this man down as childless, a man who shall not succeed in his days, for none of his offspring shall succeed in sitting on the throne of David and ruling again in Judah." (Jeremiah 22:28-30)*

This is a very important distinction to make since the first chapter of the Christian Bible claims that their *mashiach* is from this forbidden lineage of Jechoniah (Matthew 1:12).

Simply put, the *mashiach* is a human being born from the lineage of King Solomon, anointed with oil on his head as the King of Israel, and will sit on the throne of David ruling rightly before all the people in the messianic era.

How will we know who the *Mashiach* is?

Mishnah Torah, Melachim uMilchamot 10:4

> *If a king will arise from the House of David who diligently contemplates the Torah and observes its mitzvot as prescribed by the Written Law and the Oral Law as David, his ancestor, will compel all of Israel to walk in (the way of the Torah) and rectify the breaches in its*

observance, and fight the wars of G-d, we may, with assurance, consider him Mashiach.

If he succeeds in the above, builds the Temple in its place, and gathers the dispersed of Israel, he is definitely the Mashiach.

He will then improve the entire world, motivating all the nations to serve G-d together, as Tzephaniah 3:9 states: 'I will transform the peoples to a purer language that they all will call upon the name of G-d and serve Him with one purpose.'

If he did not succeed to this degree or was killed, he surely is not the redeemer promised by the Torah. Rather, he should be considered as all the other proper and complete kings of the Davidic dynasty who died. G-d caused him to arise only to test the many, as Daniel 11:35 states: 'And some of the wise men will stumble, to try them, to refine, and to clarify until the appointed time, because the set time is in the future.'

Jesus of Nazareth who aspired to be the Mashiach and was executed by the court was also alluded to in Daniel's prophecies, as ibid. 11:14 states: 'The vulgar among your people shall exalt themselves in an attempt to fulfill the vision, but they shall stumble.'

Can there be a greater stumbling block than Christianity? All the prophets spoke of Mashiach as the redeemer of Israel and their savior who would gather their dispersed and strengthen their observance of the mitzvot. In contrast, Christianity caused the Jews to be slain by the sword, their remnants to be scattered and humbled, the Torah to be altered, and the majority of the world to err and serve a god other than HaShem.

Nevertheless, the intent of the Creator of the world is not within the power of man to comprehend, for His ways are not our ways, nor are His thoughts, our thoughts. Ultimately, all the deeds of Jesus of Nazareth and that Ishmaelite who arose after him will only serve to prepare the way for Mashiach's coming and the improvement of the entire world, motivating the nations to serve G-d together as Tzephaniah 3:9 states: 'I will transform the peoples to a purer language that they all will call upon the name of G-d and serve Him with one purpose.'

How will this come about? The entire world has already become filled with the mention of Mashiach, Torah, and mitzvot. These matters have been spread to the furthermost islands to many stubborn-hearted nations. They discuss these matters and the mitzvot of the Torah, saying: 'These mitzvot were true, but were already negated in the present age and are not applicable for all time.'

Others say: 'Implied in the mitzvot are hidden concepts that cannot be understood simply. The Mashiach has already come and revealed those hidden truths.'

When the true Messianic king will arise and prove successful, his position becoming exalted and uplifted, they will all return and realize that their ancestors endowed them with a false heritage and their prophets and ancestors caused them to err.

What is the *Messianic Era?*

Mishnah Torah, Melachim uMilchamot 10:1

In the future, the Messianic king will arise and renew the Davidic dynasty, restoring it to its initial sovereignty. He will build the Temple and gather the dispersed of Israel.

Then, in his days, the observance of all the statutes will return to their previous state. We will offer sacrifices, observe the Sabbatical and Jubilee years according to all their particulars as described by the Torah.

Anyone who does not believe in him or does not await his coming, denies not only the statements of the other prophets, but those of the Torah and Moses, our teacher. The Torah testified to his coming, as Deuteronomy 30:3-5 states:

G-d will bring back your captivity and have mercy upon you. He will again gather you from among the nations... Even if your Diaspora is at the ends of the heavens, G-d will gather you up from there... and bring you to the land....

These explicit words of the Torah include all the statements made by all the prophets.

Mishnah Torah, Melachim uMilchamot 11

Do not presume that in the Messianic age any facet of the world's nature will change or there will be innovations in the work of creation. Rather, the world will continue according to its pattern.

Although Isaiah 11:6 states: 'The wolf will dwell with the lamb, the leopard will lie down with the young goat,' these words are a metaphor and a parable. The interpretation of the prophecy is as follows: Israel will dwell securely together with the wicked gentiles who are likened to a wolf and a leopard, as in the prophecy Jeremiah 5:6: 'A wolf from the wilderness shall spoil them and a leopard will stalk their cities.' They will all return to the true faith and no longer steal or destroy. Rather, they will eat permitted food at peace with Israel as Isaiah 11:7 states: 'The lion will eat straw like an ox.'

Similarly, other Messianic prophecies of this nature are metaphors. In the Messianic era, everyone will realize which matters were implied by these metaphors and which allusions they contained.

Our Sages taught: "There will be no difference between the current age and the Messianic era except the emancipation from our subjugation to the gentile kingdoms."

The simple interpretation of the prophets' words appear to imply that the war of Gog and Magog will take place at the beginning of the Messianic age. Before the war of Gog and Magog, a prophet will arise to inspire Israel to be upright and prepare their hearts, as Malachi 3:22 states: 'Behold, I am sending you Elijah.'

He will not come to declare the pure, impure, or to declare the impure, pure. He will not dispute the lineage of those presumed to be of proper pedigree, nor will he validate the pedigree of those whose lineage is presumed blemished. Rather, he will establish peace within the world as ibid. 3:24 continues: 'He will turn the hearts of the fathers to the children."

There are some Sages who say that Elijah's coming will precede the coming of the Mashiach. All these and similar matters cannot be definitely known by man until they occur for these matters are undefined in the prophets' words and even the wise men have no established tradition regarding these matters except their own interpretation of the verses. Therefore, there is a controversy among them regarding these matters.

Regardless of the debate concerning these questions, neither the order of the occurrence of these events or their precise detail are among the fundamental principles of the faith. A person should not occupy himself with the Aggadot [Tales/Lore] and homiletics concerning these and similar matters, nor should he consider them as essentials, for study of them will neither bring fear or love of G-d.

Similarly, one should not try to determine the appointed time for Mashiach's coming. Our Sages declared: 'May the spirits of those who attempt to determine the time of Mashiach's coming expire!' Rather, one *should await and believe in the general conception of the matter as explained.*

During the era of the Messianic king, once his kingdom has been established and all of Israel has gathered around him, the entire nation's line of descent will be established on the basis of his words and the prophetic spirit which will rest upon him, as Malachi 3:3 states: 'He shall sit as a refiner and purifier.'

He will purify the lineage of the Levites first, stating 'He is a priest of defined lineage. He is a Levite of defined lineage.' Those whose lineage he will not recognize will be lowered to the status of Israelites. This is implied by Ezra 2:63: 'The governor said to them: They should not eat of the most holy things until a priest arises who will wear the urim vitumim.' From this verse, you can infer that the prophetic spirit will be used to define and notify the pedigree of lineage.

When he defines the lineage of the Israelites, he will make known their tribal lineage alone, stating: 'He is from this tribe and he is from another tribe.' He will not, by contrast, state concerning a person who is presumed to be of unblemished lineage: 'He is illegitimate or he is of slave lineage.' For the law is once a family has become intermingled with the entire Jewish people, they may remain intermingled.

The Sages and the prophets did not yearn for the Messianic era in order to have dominion over the entire world, to rule over the gentiles, to be exalted by the nations, or to eat, drink, and celebrate. Rather, they desired to be free to involve themselves in Torah and wisdom without any pressures or disturbances, so that they would merit the world to come, as explained in Hilchot Teshuvah.

In that era, there will be neither famine or war, envy or competition for good will flow in abundance and all the delights will be freely available as dust. The occupation of the entire world will be solely to know G-d.

Therefore, the Jews will be great sages and know the hidden matters, grasping the knowledge of their Creator according to the full extent of human potential, as Isaiah 11:9 states: 'The world will be filled with the knowledge of G-d as the waters cover the ocean bed.'

Is *Mashiach* G-d?

It has been well known by the righteous since Adam that G-d is not a man.

G-d is not a man to be capricious, or mortal to change his mind.
(Numbers 23:19)

If one believes in the one true G-d of Israel, he can't believe a man, even *Mashiach*, is G-d. Belief that the *Mashiach* can be G-d, heaven forbid, is a direct violation of the Noahide Laws, but also goes against the majority of The Thirteen Principles of Jewish Faith.

The Thirteen Principles of Jewish Faith

1. Belief in the existence of the Creator, who is perfect in every manner of existence and is the Primary Cause of all that exists.

2. The belief in G-d's absolute and unparalleled unity.

3. The belief in G-d's non-corporeality, nor that He will be affected by any physical occurrences, such as movement, or rest, or dwelling.

4. The belief in G-d's eternity.

5. The imperative to worship G-d exclusively and no foreign false gods.

6. The belief that G-d communicates with man through prophecy.

7. The belief in the primacy of the prophecy of Moses our teacher.

8. The belief in the divine origin of the Torah.

9. The belief in the immutability of the Torah.

10. The belief in G-d's omniscience and providence.

11. The belief in divine reward and retribution.

12. The belief in the arrival of the Messiah and the messianic era.

13. The belief in the resurrection of the dead.

G-d existed before anything physical, so to call wood, stone, living beings, or dirt (including man who was formed form dirt) G-d is idolatry. He exists eternally before man's creation and would continue to exist if man never existed. Therefore, he can't be a man which is dependent upon G-d to exist.

G-d is so perfect in his unity that it is impossible to even imagine that he has any distinct parts or members like a human body. Therefore, even the idea of a duplicitous or trinitarian G-d is impossible.

G-d is completely unified at all times in all ways, indistinguishable from himself and unchanging eternally. Even if one were to form an image of G-d in his imagination, G-d forbid, it is most certainly not the One of which is said, "*Shema Israel HaShem Elokeinu HaShem echad.*"

G-d eternally exists outside of any physicality. He neither sleeps nor eats. He doesn't grow tired or become sad. To imply that He does these corporeal things would be to say that G-d changes, which he does not. G-d was not born, nor can he die. He can't be beaten with whips or cry out in pain.

Any such occurrence in the *Tenakh* where physical imagery is attributed to him is purely allegorical imagery that the human mind can understand, and not to be taken literally as if G-d is a physical being such as a man.

G-d is above all creation, so if one elevates *Mashiach* to the status of being G-d, he elevates him above the primacy of the prophecy of Moses our teacher. The *Mashiach* may possibly be more highly exalted than Moses in the future, but he most certainly does not have primacy over the prophesy of Moses our teacher.

HaShem said to Moses, "Behold! I come to you in the thickness of the cloud, so that the people will hear as I speak to you, and they will also believe in you forever." (Exodus 19:9)

If one believes in the one true G-d of Israel, he can't believe *Mashiach* was, is, or ever will be G-d. Anyone who worships an entity that varies even slightly from these parameters is in violation of the universal instruction to worship G-d exclusively.

Most of the content of this section falls under the umbrella of the 1ˢᵗ Noahide Law we expanded previously. See *Noahide Laws* for more clarification on what Judaism teaches about G-d.

Can *Mashiach* die for sins?

The *Tenakh* strictly forbids any man from being punished for another man's sins and is very specific over and over that only the soul who sins shall die. It is not transferrable, and to treat sin as transferable is boldly against the Torah. To punish oneself for another's sins is a violation of many commandments, not the least of which is to uphold justice.

Also, human sacrifice is strictly forbidden and is considered an explicit abominable form of idolatry.

It is unjust to punish one man for another man's sins. Rather, each person should take responsibility for his own shortcomings and repent so that he may live.

Much is written about this topic in the *Tenakh*, so only a small amount will be quoted here regarding this topic.

Fathers shall not be put to death because of sons, and sons shall not be put to death because of fathers; a man should be put to death for his own sin. (Deuteronomy 24:16)

Ezekiel 18

1The word of the L-RD came to me: 2"What do you mean by repeating this proverb concerning the land of Israel, 'The fathers have eaten sour grapes, and the children's teeth are set on edge'? 3As I live, declares the L-rd G-D, this proverb shall no more be used by you in Israel. 4Behold, all souls are mine; the soul of the father as well as the soul of the son is mine: the soul who sins shall die.

5"If a man is righteous and does what is just and right— 6if he does not eat upon the mountains or lift up his eyes to the idols of the house of Israel, does not defile his neighbor's wife or approach a woman in her time of menstrual impurity, 7does not oppress anyone, but restores to the debtor his pledge, commits no robbery, gives his bread to the hungry and covers the naked with a garment, 8does not lend at interest or take any profit, withholds his hand from injustice, executes true justice between man and man, 9walks in my statutes, and keeps my rules by acting faithfully—he is righteous; he shall surely live, declares the L-rd G-D.

10"If he fathers a son who is violent, a shedder of blood, who does any of these things 11(though he himself did none of these things), who even eats upon the mountains, defiles his neighbor's wife, 12oppresses the poor and needy, commits robbery, does not restore the pledge, lifts up his eyes to the idols, commits abomination, 13lends at interest, and takes profit; shall he then live? He shall not live. He has done all these abominations; he shall surely die; his blood shall be upon himself.

14"Now suppose this man fathers a son who sees all the sins that his father has done; he sees, and does not do likewise:15he does not eat upon the mountains or lift up his eyes to the idols of the house of Israel, does not defile his neighbor's wife,16does not oppress anyone, exacts no pledge, commits no robbery, but gives his bread to the hungry and covers the naked with a garment, 17withholds his hand from iniquity, takes no interest or profit, obeys my rules, and walks in my statutes; he shall not die for his father's iniquity; he shall surely live. 18As for his father, because he practiced extortion, robbed his brother, and did what is not good among his people, behold, he shall die for his iniquity.

19"Yet you say, 'Why should not the son suffer for the iniquity of the father?' When the son has done what is just and right, and has been careful to observe all my statutes, he shall surely live. 20The soul who sins shall die. The son shall not suffer for the iniquity of the father, nor the father suffer for the iniquity of the son. The righteousness of the righteous shall be upon himself, and the wickedness of the wicked shall be upon himself.

21"But if a wicked person turns away from all his sins that he has committed and keeps all my statutes and does what is just and right, he shall surely live; he shall not die. 22None of the transgressions that he has committed shall be remembered against him; for the righteousness that he has done he shall live. 23Have I any pleasure in the death of the wicked, declares the L-rd G-D, and not rather that he should turn from his way and live? 24But when a righteous person turns away from his righteousness and does injustice and does the same abominations that the wicked person does, shall he live? None of the righteous deeds that he has done shall be remembered; for the treachery of which he is guilty and the sin he has committed, for them he shall die.

25"Yet you say, 'The way of the L-rd is not just.' Hear now, O house of Israel: Is my way not just? Is it not your ways that are not just? 26When a righteous person turns away from his righteousness and does injustice, he shall die for it; for the injustice that he has done he shall die. 27Again, when a wicked person turns away from the wickedness he has committed and does what is just and right, he shall save his life. 28Because he considered and turned away from all the transgressions that he had committed, he shall surely live; he shall not die. 29Yet the house of Israel says, 'The way of the L-rd is not just.' O house of Israel, are my ways not just? Is it not your ways that are not just?

30"Therefore I will judge you, O house of Israel, every one according to his ways, declares the L-rd G-D. Repent and turn from all your transgressions, lest iniquity be your ruin. 31Cast away from you all the transgressions that you have committed, and make yourselves a new heart and a new spirit! Why will you die, O house of Israel? 32For I have no pleasure in the death of anyone, declares the L-rd G-D; so turn, and live."

Is *Mashiach* the Passover lamb?

Christianity ties the idea of *Mashiach* to the Passover lamb as a sacrifice for sins. Judaism does not claim the *Mashiach* is the Pesach. Again, HaShem strictly prohibits human sacrifice.

One of the problems with this Christian doctrine is that the Passover lamb was not for sin, but rather the blood was used to redeem the firstborn sons and animals of each household, and they ate Passover lamb in haste.

If the Passover lamb was for sin, this would mean that G-d punished the firstborn child and animal in each household for the sins of the entire family, or G-d punished only the firstborn sons and animals for their own sins. It is strictly forbidden to punish a son for the sins of the father.

> *Fathers shall not be put to death because of sons, and sons shall not be put to death because of fathers; a man should be put to death for his own sin. (Deuteronomy 24:16)*

The Passover was a fulfillment of the *Akedah* (Genesis 22), when Abraham brought Isaac onto Mt. Moriah, and his faith sealed the promise that the future nation of Israel would be G-d's first born son.

The first born sons and animals of Israel have been required to be redeemed ever since the Passover.

> *'It shall be, when HaShem shall bring you into the land of the Kana`ani, as he swore to you and to your fathers, and shall give it you, that you shall set apart to HaShem all that opens the womb, and every firstborn which you have that comes from an animal. The males shall be HaShem's. Every firstborn of a donkey you shall redeem with a lamb; and if you will not redeem it, then you shall break its neck; and you shall redeem all the*

firstborn of man among your sons. It shall be, when your son asks you in time to come, saying, 'What is this?' that you shall tell him, 'By strength of hand HaShem brought us out from Mitzrayim (Egypt), from the house of bondage; and it happened, when Par`oh would hardly let us go, that HaShem killed all the firstborn in the land of Mitzrayim, both the firstborn of man, and the firstborn of animal. Therefore I sacrifice to HaShem all that opens the womb, being males; but all the firstborn of my sons I redeem.' (Exodus 13:11-15)

The Passover lamb was never about paying for sins, but redeeming the nation of Israel as the firstborn son of HaShem.

When will *Mashiach* come?

Hopefully now! Or maybe...NOW! Well, at least that is what we all hope for.

Mishnah Torah, Melachim uMilchamot 11:2

Similarly, one should not try to determine the appointed time for Mashiach's coming. Our Sages declared: 'May the spirits of those who attempt to determine the time of Mashiach's coming expire!' Rather, one should await and believe in the general conception of the matter as explained.

There is also the concept that *Mashiach* is present in every generation. It is a fundamental belief that we must expect the coming of *Mashiach* every day. Therefore, there must be a righteous one among us from the lineage of Judah in every generation.

Maybe he will come... NOW! We will continue to expect him every day!

TRUE or FALSE

1. One should not use the information in this book to harm his neighbor.
2. Christianity teaches that G-d is a man.
3. *Mashach* means "to anoint" with oil by pouring of the top.
4. The word *mashiach* appears 39 times in the *Tenakh.*
5. *Mashiach* refers to a King or High Priest of Israel who is anointed into their position by a legitimate prophet of G-d pouring oil over his head.
6. The High Priest is also called the *Kohen HaMashiach* (Anointed Priest).
7. The King of Israel is also called the *Melech HaMashiach* (Anointed King).
8. The first *Kohen HaMashiach* was Aaron.
9. The first *Melech HaMashiach* was King Saul.
10. It is impossible for a man to be both *Kohen HaMashiach* and *Melech HaMashiach.*
11. The *Mashiach* can't be from the lineage of Jechoniah, the King of Judah that surrendered Israel into the Babylonian captivity.
12. The first chapter of the Christian Bible identifies their *mashiach* as a descendant of Jechoniah.
13. *Mashiach* will come through the lineage of King David's son, King Solomon.
14. *Mashiach* will diligently contemplate the Torah and observe its *mitzvot* as prescribed by the Written Torah and *Torah Shebaal Peh* (Oral Torah).
15. *Mashiach* will compel all of Israel to walk in the way of the Torah.

16. *Mashiach* will rectify the breaches in the observance of the Torah.

17. *Mashiach* will fight the wars of G-d.

18. *Mashiach* will build the Temple in its place.

19. *Mashiach* will gather the dispersed of Israel.

20. *Mashiach* will improve the entire world, motivating all the nations to serve G-d together.

21. If a man dies before accomplishing all of the things to the full degree that *Mashiach* is prophesied to do them, he is definitely not *Mashiach*.

22. Jesus of Nazareth (or any other way his name is pronounced) aspired to be *Mashiach,* but stumbled and was executed.

23. In contrast to the prophesies about *Mashiach* in the *Tenakh,* the legacy of Jesus of Nazereth is that of millions of Jews repeatedly slain by the sword, scattered, and stumbling in their observance of the *mitzvot;* the Torah altered; and the majority of the world to err and serve a god other than HaShem.

24. Christianity and Islam have filled the world with the mention of *Mashiach, Torah,* and *mitzvot.*

25. When *Mashiach* is revealed, the Christians and Muslims throughout the whole world will realize their ancestors endowed them with a false heritage and their prophets and ancestor caused them to err.

26. The *Messianic Era* is the era when *Mashiach* will build the Temple and gather the dispersed of Israel.

27. The observance of all the statutes as observed in the diaspora will return to their previous state in the *Messianic Era.*

28. Anyone who does not believe in *Mashiach* or await his coming denies the Torah and Moses, our teacher.

29. Our Sages taught that there will be no difference between the current age and the *Messianic Era* except the emancipation

of the sons of Jacob from their subjugation to the gentile kingdoms.

30. The war of Gog and Magog will most likely take place at the beginning of the Messianic Era.

31. One should not occupy himself with the Aggadot and homiletics concerning the order of events in the *Messianic Era,* the appointed time for *Mashiac's* coming, or similar matters.

32. *Mashiach* will make known the tribal lineage of the Israelites stating, "He is from this tribe and he is from another tribe."

33. *Mashiach* will purify the lineage of the Levites first.

34. There will be no famine, war, envy, or competition in the *Messianic Era.*

35. In the *Messianic Era,* the entire world will be occupied solely with knowing G-d.

36. No man can ever be G-d, not even *Mashiach,* and believing a man is G-d is forbidden by the Torah for all people.

37. There are thirteen principles of Jewish faith.

38. *Mashiach* will not be elevated above the primacy of the prophesy of Moses our teacher.

39. G-d can't die or be punished.

40. The Torah strictly forbids a man to be punished for another man's sins, even if that man is his son or father.

41. The soul who sins will die, and the soul who repents will live.

42. The Passover lamb was not sacrificed for sin, but to redeem the firstborn sons and livestock of Israel.

43. Israel is G-d's firstborn son.

44. The coming of *Mashiach* is imminent.

45. *Mashiach* is present on the earth in every generation, even now.

ANSWERS

All answers are TRUE.

TESHUVAH

TESHUVAH IS A CORE PRINCIPLE of Judaism. *Teshuvah* means to "repent." Living in a world of idolatry can profoundly affect how one views repentance and forgiveness. This chapter will give you the basic knowledge necessary to understand atonement and forgiveness for sins.

Some subjects are so important to understand, merely summarizing the knowledge takes away from important aspects of the text. *Teshuvah* is one of those subjects.

Confession & Atonement
(Hilchos Teshuvah 1)

1 If a person transgresses any of the mitzvot of the Torah, whether a positive command or a negative command - whether willingly or inadvertently - when he repents, and returns from his sin, he must confess before G-d, blessed be He, as [Numbers 5:6-7] states: "If a man or a woman commit any of the sins of man... they must confess the sin that they committed."

This refers to a verbal confession. This confession is a positive command.

How does one confess: He states: "I implore You, G-d, I sinned, I transgressed, I committed iniquity before You by doing the following. Behold, I regret and am embarrassed for my deeds. I promise never to repeat this act again."

These are the essential elements of the confessional prayer. Whoever confesses profusely and elaborates on these matters is worthy of praise.

Those who bring sin offerings or guilt offerings must also [confess their sins] when they bring their sacrifices for their inadvertent or willful transgressions. Their sacrifices will not atone for their sins until they repent and make a verbal confession as [Leviticus 5:5] states: "He shall confess the sin he has committed upon it."

Similarly, those obligated to be executed or lashed by the court do not attain atonement through their death or lashing unless they repent and confess. Similarly, someone who injures a colleague or damages his property, does not attain atonement, even though he pays him what he owes until he confesses and makes a commitment never to do such a thing again as implied by the phrase [Numbers, loc. cit..], "any of the sins of man."

2 Since the goat sent [to Azazel] atones for all of Israel, the High Priest confesses upon it as a spokesman for all of Israel as [Leviticus 16:21] states: "He shall confess upon it all the sins of the children of Israel."

The goat sent to Azazel atones for all the transgressions in the Torah, the severe and the lighter [sins]; those violated intentionally and those transgressed inadvertently; those which [the transgressor] became conscious of and those which he was not conscious of. All are atoned for by the goat sent [to Azazel].

This applies only if one repents. If one does not repent, the goat only atones for the light [sins].

Which are light sins and which are severe ones? The severe sins are those for which one is liable for execution by the court or karet [cut off]. False and unnecessary oaths are also considered severe sins even though they are not [punished by] karet. [The violation of] the other prohibitions and [the failure to perform] positive commandments that are not punishable by karet are considered light [sins].

3 At present, when the Temple does not exist and there is no altar of atonement, there remains nothing else aside from Teshuvah.

Teshuvah atones for all sins. Even a person who was wicked his whole life and repented in his final moments will not be reminded of any aspect of his wickedness as [Ezekiel 33:12] states "the wickedness of the evil one will not cause him to stumble on the day he repents his wickedness."

The essence of Yom Kippur atones for those who repent as [Leviticus 16:30] states: "This day will atone for you."

4 Even though Teshuvah atones for all [sins] and the essence of Yom Kippur brings atonement, [there are different levels of sin and hence, differences in the degree of atonement.] There are sins that can be atoned for immediately and other sins which can only be atoned for over the course of time. What is implied?

If a person violates a positive command which is not punishable by karet and repents, he will not leave that place before he is forgiven. Concerning these sins, [Jeremiah 3:22] states: "Return, faithless children! I will heal your rebellious acts."

If a person violates a prohibition that is not punishable by karet or execution by the court and repents, Teshuvah has a tentative effect and Yom Kippur brings atonement as [Leviticus, loc. cit. states "This day will atone for you."

If a person violates [sins punishable by] karet or execution by the court and repents, Teshuvah and Yom Kippur have a tentative effect and the sufferings which come upon him complete the atonement. He will never achieve complete atonement until he endures suffering for concerning these [sins, Psalms 89:33] states: "I will punish their transgression with a rod."

When does the above apply: When the desecration of G-d's name is not involved in the transgression. However, a person who desecrated G-d's name, even though he repented, Yom Kippur arrived while he continued his repentance, and he experienced suffering, will not be granted complete atonement until he dies. The three: repentance, Yom Kippur, and suffering have a tentative effect and death atones as [Isaiah 22:14] states: "It was revealed in my ears [by] the L-rd of Hosts, surely this iniquity will not be atoned for until you die."

Complete Teshuvah
(Hilchos Teshuvah 2)

1 [Who has reached] complete Teshuvah? A person who confronts the same situation in which he sinned when he has the potential to commit [the sin again], and, nevertheless, abstains and does not commit it because of his Teshuvah alone and not because of fear or a lack of strength.

For example, a person engaged in illicit sexual relations with a woman. Afterwards, they met in privacy, in the same country, while his love for her and physical power still persisted, and nevertheless, he abstained and did not transgress. This is a complete Baal-Teshuvah. This was implied by King Solomon in his statement [Ecclesiastes 12:1] "Remember your Creator in the days of your youth, [before the bad days come and the years draw near when you will say: `I have no desire for them.'"]

If he does not repent until his old age, at a time when he is incapable of doing what he did before, even though this is not a high level of repentance, he is a Baal-Teshuvah.

Even if he transgressed throughout his entire life and repented on the day of his death and died in repentance, all his sins are forgiven as [Ecclesiastes, op. cit.:2] continues: "Before the sun, the light, the moon, or the stars are darkened and the clouds return after the rain..." - This refers to the day of death. Thus, we can infer that if one remembers his Creator and repents before he dies, he is forgiven.

2 What constitutes Teshuvah? That a sinner should abandon his sins and remove them from his thoughts, resolving in his heart, never to commit them again as [Isaiah 55:7] states "May the wicked abandon his ways...." Similarly, he must regret the past as [Jeremiah 31:18] states: "After I returned, I regretted."

[He must reach the level where] He who knows the hidden will testify concerning him that he will never return to this sin again as [Hoshea 14:4] states: "We will no longer say to the work of our hands: `You are our gods.'"

He must verbally confess and state these matters which he resolved in his heart.

3 Anyone who verbalizes his confession without resolving in his heart to abandon [sin] can be compared to [a person] who immerses himself [in a mikvah] while [holding the carcass of] a lizard in his hand. His immersion will not be of avail until he casts away the carcass.

This principle is implied by the statement, [Proverbs 28:13], "He who confesses and forsakes [his sins] will be treated with mercy."

It is necessary to mention particularly one's sins as evidenced by [Moses' confession, Exodus 32:31]: "I appeal to You. The people have committed a terrible sin by making a golden idol."

4 Among the paths of repentance is for the penitent to

a) constantly call out before G-d, crying and entreating;

b) to perform charity according to his potential;

c) to separate himself far from the object of his sin;

d) to change his name, as if to say "I am a different person and not the same one who sinned;"

e) to change his behavior in its entirety to the good and the path of righteousness; and

f) to travel in exile from his home. Exile atones for sin because it causes a person to be submissive, humble, and meek of spirit.

5 It is very praiseworthy for a person who repents to confess in public and to make his sins known to others, revealing the transgressions he committed against his colleagues.

He should tell them: "Though I sinned against so and so, committing the following misdeeds.... Behold, I repent and express my regret." Anyone who, out of pride, conceals his sins and does not reveal them will not achieve complete repentance as [Proverbs 28:13] states: "He who conceals his sins will not succeed."

When does the above apply? In regard to sins between man and man. However, in regard to sins between man and G-d, it is not necessary to publicize one's [transgressions]. Indeed, revealing them is arrogant. Rather, a person should repent before G-d, blessed be He, and specifically mention his sins before Him. In public, he should make a general confession. It is to his benefit not to reveal his sins as [Psalms 32:1] states: "Happy is he whose transgression is forgiven, whose sin is covered."

6 Even though repentance and calling out [to G-d] are desirable at all times, during the ten days between Rosh HaShanah and Yom Kippur, they are even more desirable and will be accepted immediately as [Isaiah 55:6] states: "Seek G-d when He is to be found."

When does the above apply? To an individual. However, in regard to a community, whenever they repent and cry out wholeheartedly, they are answered immediately as [Deuteronomy 4:7] states: "[What nation is so great that they have G-d close to them,] as G-d, our L-rd, is whenever we call Him."

7 Yom Kippur is the time of Teshuvah for all, both individuals and the community at large. It is the apex of forgiveness and pardon for Israel. Accordingly, everyone is obligated to repent and confess on Yom Kippur.

The mitzvah of the confession of Yom Kippur begins on the day's eve, before one eats [the final meal], lest one choke to death in the meal before confessing.

Although a person confessed before eating, he should confess again in the evening service, Yom Kippur night, and similarly, repeat the confession in the morning, Musaf, afternoon, and Ne'ilah services.

At which point [in the service] should one confess? An individual confesses after the Amidah and the Chazan confesses in the midst of the Amidah, in the fourth blessing.

8 The confessional prayer customarily recited by all Israel is: "For we have all sinned...." This is the essence of the confessional prayer. Sins which were confessed on one Yom Kippur should be confessed on another Yom Kippur even though one remains steadfast in his repentance, as [Psalms 51:5] states: "I acknowledge my transgressions and my sins are always before me."

9 Teshuvah and Yom Kippur only atone for sins between man and G-d; for example, a person who ate a forbidden food or engaged in forbidden sexual relations, and the like. However, sins between man and man; for example, someone who injures a colleague, curses a colleague, steals from him, or the like will never be forgiven until he gives his colleague what he owes him and appeases him.

[It must be emphasized that] even if a person restores the money that he owes [the person he wronged], he must appease him and ask him to forgive him.

Even if a person only upset a colleague by saying [certain] things, he must appease him and approach him [repeatedly] until he forgives him.

If his colleague does not desire to forgive him, he should bring a group of three of his friends and approach him with them and request [forgiveness]. If [the wronged party] is not appeased, he should repeat the process a second and third time. If he [still] does not want [to forgive him], he may let him alone and need not pursue [the matter further]. On the contrary, the person who refuses to grant forgiveness is the one considered as the sinner.

[The above does not apply] if [the wronged party] was one's teacher. [In that instance,] a person should continue seeking his forgiveness, even a thousand times, until he forgives him.

10 It is forbidden for a person to be cruel and refuse to be appeased. Rather, he should be easily pacified, but hard to anger. When the person who wronged him asks for forgiveness, he should forgive him with a complete heart and a willing spirit. Even if he aggravated and wronged him severely, he should not seek revenge or bear a grudge.

This is the path of the seed of Israel and their upright spirit. In contrast, the insensitive gentiles do not act in this manner. Rather, their wrath is preserved forever. Similarly, because the Gibeonites did not forgive and refused to be appeased, [II Samuel 21:2] describes them, as follows: "The Gibeonites are not among the children of Israel."

11 If a person wronged a colleague and the latter died before he could ask him for forgiveness, he should take ten people and say the following while they are standing before the colleague's grave: "I sinned against G-d, the L-rd of Israel, and against this person by doing the following to him...."

If he owed him money, he should return it to his heirs. If he is unaware of the identity of his heirs, he should place [the sum] in [the hands of] the court and confess.

Divine Reward & Retribution

(Hilchos Teshuvah 3:1-5)

1 Each and every person has merits and sins. A person whose merits exceed his sins is [termed] righteous. A person whose sins exceed his merits is [termed] wicked. If [his sins and merits] are equal, he is termed a Beinoni.

The same applies to an entire country. If the merits of all its inhabitants exceed their sins, it is [termed] righteous. If their sins are greater, it is [termed] wicked. The same applies to the entire world.

2 If a person's sins exceed his merits, he will immediately die because of his wickedness as [Jeremiah 30:14] states: "[I have smitten you...] for the multitude of your transgressions."

Similarly, a country whose sins are great will immediately be obliterated as implied by [Genesis 18:20]: "The outcry of Sodom and Amorah is great....

In regard to the entire world as well, were its [inhabitants'] sins to be greater than their merits, they would immediately be destroyed as [Genesis 6:5] relates: "G-d saw the evil of man was great... [and G-d said: `I will destroy man....']"

This reckoning is not calculated [only] on the basis of the number of merits and sins, but also [takes into account] their magnitude. There are some merits which outweigh many sins as implied by [I Kings 14:13]: "Because in him, there was found a good quality." In contrast, a sin may outweigh many merits as [Ecclesiastes 9:18] states: "One sin may obscure much good."

The weighing [of sins and merits] is carried out according to the wisdom of the Knowing G-d. He knows how to measure merits against sins.

3 Anyone who changes his mind about the mitzvot he has performed and regrets the merits [he has earned], saying in his heart: "What value was there in doing them? I wish I hadn't performed them" - loses them all and no merit is preserved for him at all as [Ezekiel 33:12] states "The righteousness of the upright will not save him on the day of his transgression." This only applies to one who regrets his previous [deeds].

Just as a person's merits and sins are weighed at the time of his death, so, too, the sins of every inhabitant of the world together with his merits are weighed on the festival of Rosh HaShanah. If one is found righteous, his [verdict] is sealed for life. If one is found wicked, his [verdict] is sealed for death. A Beinoni's verdict remains tentative until Yom Kippur. If he repents, his [verdict] is sealed for life. If not, his [verdict] is sealed for death.

4 Even though the sounding of the shofar on Rosh HaShanah is a decree, it contains an allusion. It is as if [the shofar's call] is saying:

Wake up you sleepy ones from your sleep and you who slumber, arise. Inspect your deeds, repent, remember your Creator. Those who forget the truth in the vanities of time and throughout the entire year, devote their energies to vanity and emptiness which will not benefit or save: Look to your souls. Improve your ways and your deeds and let every one of you abandon his evil path and thoughts.

Accordingly, throughout the entire year, a person should always look at himself as equally balanced between merit and sin and the world as equally balanced between merit and sin. If he performs one sin, he tips his balance and that of the entire world to the side of guilt and brings destruction upon himself.

[On the other hand,] if he performs one mitzvah, he tips his balance and that of the entire world to the side of merit and brings deliverance and salvation to himself and others. This is implied by [Proverbs 10:25] "A righteous man is the foundation of the world," i.e., he who acted righteously, tipped the balance of the entire world to merit and saved it.

For these reasons, it is customary for all of Israel to give profusely to charity, perform many good deeds, and be occupied with mitzvot from Rosh HaShanah until Yom Kippur to a greater extent than during the remainder of the year.

During these ten days, the custom is for everyone to rise [while it is still] night and pray in the synagogues with heart-rending words of supplication until daybreak.

5 When a person's sins are being weighed against his merits, [G-d] does not count a sin that was committed only once or twice. [A sin] is only [counted] if it was committed three times or more.

Should it be found that [even] those sins committed more than three times outweigh a person's merits, the sins that were committed twice [or less] are also added and he is judged for all of his sins.

If his merits are equal to [or greater than the amount of] his sins committed which were committed more than three times, [G-d] forgives his sins one after the other, i.e., the third sin [is forgiven because] it is considered as a first sin, for the two previous sins were already forgiven. Similarly, after the third sin is forgiven, the fourth sin is considered as a "first" [sin and is forgiven according to the same principle].

The same [pattern is continued] until [all his sins] are concluded.

When does the above apply? In regard to an individual as can be inferred from [Job 33:29] "All these things, G-d will do twice or three times with a man." However, in regard to a community, [retribution for] the first, second, and third sins is held in abeyance as implied by [Amos 2:6] "For three sins of Israel, [I will withhold retribution,] but for the fourth, I will not withhold it." When a reckoning [of their merits and sins] is made according to the above pattern, the reckoning begins with the fourth [sin].

[As mentioned above,] a Beinoni [is one whose scale is equally balanced between merit and sin]. However, if among his sins is [the neglect of the mitzvah of] tefillin [to the extent that] he never wore them even once, *he is judged according to his sins. He will, nevertheless, be granted a portion in the world to come.*

Similarly, all the wicked whose sins are greater [than their merits] are judged according to their sins, but they are granted a portion in the world to come for all Israel have a share in the world to come as [Isaiah 60:21] states "Your people are all righteous, they shall inherit the land forever." "The land" is an analogy alluding to "the land of life," i.e., the world to come. Similarly, the "pious of the nations of the world" have a portion in the world to come.

(Hilchos Teshuvah 3:14)

When does the statement that these individuals do not have a portion in the world to come apply? When they die without having repented. However, if such a person repents from his wicked deeds and dies as a Baal-Teshuvah, he will merit the world to come, for nothing can stand in the way of Teshuvah.

Even if he denies G-d's existence throughout his life and repents in his final moments, he merits a portion in the world to come as implied by [Isaiah 57:19] "`Peace, peace, to the distant and the near,' declares G-d. `I will heal him.'"

Any wicked person, apostate, or the like, who repents, whether in an open, revealed manner or in private, will be accepted as implied by [Jeremiah 3:22] "Return, faithless children." [We may infer] that even if one is still faithless, as obvious from the fact that he repents in private and not in public, his Teshuvah will be accepted.

Free Will

(Hilchos Teshuvah 5:1)

Free will is granted to all men. If one desires to turn himself to the path of good and be righteous, the choice is his. Should he desire to turn to the path of evil and be wicked, the choice is his.

This is [the intent of] the Torah's statement (Genesis 3:22): "Behold, man has become unique as ourselves, knowing good and evil," i.e., the human species became singular in the world with no other species resembling it in the following quality: that man can, on his own initiative, with his knowledge and thought, know good and evil, and do what he desires. There is no one who can prevent him from doing good or bad. Accordingly, [there was a need to drive him from the Garden of Eden,] "lest he stretch out his hand [and take from the tree of life]."

(Hilchos Teshuvah 6:5)

What was implied by David's statement [Psalms 25:8-9]: "G-d is good and upright, therefore, he instructs sinners in the path. He guides the humble [in the path of justice and] teaches the humble His way]"? That He sends them prophets to inform them of the path of G-d and to encourage them to repent.

Furthermore, it implies that He granted them the power to learn and to understand. This attribute is present in all men: As long as a person follows the ways of wisdom and righteousness, he will desire them and pursue them. This [may be inferred from] the statement of our Sages of blessed memory: "One who comes to purify [himself] is helped;" i.e., he finds himself assisted in this matter.

Drawing Near
(Hilchos Teshuvah 7)

1 Since free choice is granted to all men as explained, a person should always strive to do Teshuvah and to confess verbally for his sins, striving to cleanse his hands from sin in order that he may die as a Baal-Teshuvah and merit the life of the world to come.

2 A person should always view himself as leaning towards death, with the possibility that he might die at any time. Thus, he may be found as a sinner.

Therefore, one should always repent from his sins immediately and should not say: "When I grow older, I will repent," for perhaps he will die before he grows older. This was implied by the wise counsel given by Solomon [Ecclesiastes 9:8]: "At all times, your clothes should be white."

3 A person should not think that repentance is only necessary for those sins that involve deed such as promiscuity, robbery, or theft. Rather, just as a person is obligated to repent from these, similarly, he must search after the evil character traits he has. He must repent from anger, hatred, envy, frivolity, the pursuit of money and honor, the pursuit of gluttony, and the like. He must repent for all [of the above].

These sins are more difficult than those that involve deed. If a person is attached to these, it is more difficult for him to separate himself. In this context, [Isaiah 55:7] exhorts: "May the wicked abandon his path and the crooked man, his designs."

4 A Baal-Teshuvah should not consider himself distant from the level of the righteous because of the sins and transgressions that he committed. This is not true. He is beloved and desirable before the Creator as if he never sinned.

Furthermore, he has a great reward for he has tasted sin and yet, separated himself from it, conquering his [evil] inclination. Our Sages declared: "In the place where Baalei Teshuvah stand, even the completely righteous are not able to stand." The level of Baalei Teshuvah transcends the level of those who never sinned at all, for they overcome their [evil] inclination more.

5 All the prophets commanded [the people] to repent. Israel will only be redeemed through Teshuvah.

The Torah has already promised that, ultimately, Israel will repent towards the end of her exile and, immediately, she will be redeemed as [Deuteronomy 30:1-3] states: "There shall come a time when [you will experience] all these things... and you will return to G-d, your L-rd.... G-d, your L-rd, will bring back your [captivity]."

6 Teshuvah is great for it draws a man close to the Shechinah as [Hoshea 14:2] states: "Return, O Israel, to G-d, your L-rd;" [Amos 4:6] states: "`You have not returned to Me,' declares G-d;" and [Jeremiah 4:1] states: "`If, you will return, 0 Israel,' declares G-d, `You will return to Me.'" Implied is that if you will return in Teshuvah, you will cling to Me.

Teshuvah brings near those who were far removed. Previously, this person was hated by G-d, disgusting, far removed, and abominable. Now, he is beloved and desirable, close, and dear.

Similarly, we find G-d employs the same expression with which He separates [Himself] from the sinners to draw close those who repent. [Hoshea 2:1] states: "Instead of saying to you: `You are not My nation,' He will tell you: `You are the children of the living G-d.'"

[Also, Jeremiah] speaks of Yecheniah while he was wicked [with the expression (22:30)]: "Write down this man as childless, a man who shall never prosper in his days," and [22:24]: "Would Cheniah, the son of Yehoyakim, king of Judah, be the signet ring on My right hand, I would tear him off." However, after he repented when in exile, [Chaggai 2:23] said concerning Zerubavel, his son: "'On that day,' declares the G-d of Hosts, `I will take you, Zerubavel, the son of Shaltiel, My servant,' declares G-d, `and I will place you as a signet ring.'"

7 How exalted is the level of Teshuvah! Previously, the [transgressor] was separate from G-d, the L-rd of Israel, as [Isaiah 59:2] states: "Your sins separate between you and your G-d." He would call out [to G-d] without being answered as [Isaiah 1:15] states: "Even if you pray many times, I will not hear."

He would fulfill mitzvot, only to have them crushed before him as [Isaiah 1:12] states: "Who asked this from you, to trample in My courts," and [Malachi 1:10] states: "`O were there one among you who would shut the doors that you might not kindle fire on My altar for no reason! I have no pleasure in you,' says the G-d of Hosts, `nor will I accept an offering from your hand.'"

Now, he is clinging to the Shechinah as [Deuteronomy 4:4] states: "And you who cling to G-d, your L-rd." He calls out [to G-d] and is answered immediately as [Isaiah 65:24] states: "Before, you will call out, I will answer." He fulfills mitzvot and they are accepted with pleasure and joy as [Ecclesiastes 9:7] states, "G-d has already accepted your works," and [Malachi 3:4] states: "Then, shall the offering of Judah and Jerusalem be pleasing to G-d as in days of old and as in the former years."

8 The manner of Baalei Teshuvah is to be very humble and modest.

If fools shame them because of their previous deeds, saying to them: "Yesterday, you would commit such and such [sins]. Yesterday, you would commit these and these [transgressions]," they will pay no attention to them. On the contrary, they will hear [this abuse] and rejoice, knowing that it is a merit for them.

Whenever they are embarrassed for the deeds they committed and shamed because of them, their merit increases and their level is raised.

It is an utter sin to tell a Baal Teshuvah, "Remember your previous deeds," or to recall them in his presence to embarrass him or to mention the surrounding circumstances or other similar matters so that he will recall what he did. This is all forbidden. We are warned against it within the general category of verbal abuse which Torah has warned us against as [Leviticus 25:17] states: "A man should not mistreat his colleague."

Olam Habah (The World to Come)

(Hilchos Teshuvah 8)

1 The good that is hidden for the righteous is the life of the world to come. This will be life which is not accompanied by death and good which is not accompanied by evil. The Torah alludes to this in [the promise, Deuteronomy 22:7]: "So that good will be granted you and you will live long."

The oral tradition explains: "So that good will be granted you" - in the world that is entirely good; "and you will live long" - in the world which is endlessly long, the world to come.

The reward of the righteous is that they will merit this pleasure and take part in this good. The retribution of the wicked is that they will not merit this life. Rather, they will be cut off and die.

Whoever does not merit this life is [truly] dead and will not live forever. Rather, he will be cut off in his wickedness and perish as a beast. This is the intent of the meaning of the term karet in the Torah as [Numbers 15:31] states: "That soul shall surely be cut off."

[Based on the repetition of the verb,] the oral tradition explains: hikaret means to be cut off in this world and tikaret, to be cut off in the world to come. After these souls become separated from bodies in this world, they will not merit the life of the world to come. Rather, even in the world to come, they will be cut off.

2 In the world to come, there is no body or physical form, only the souls of the righteous alone, without a body, like the ministering angels. Since there is no physical form, there is neither eating, drinking, nor any of the other bodily functions of this world like sitting, standing, sleeping, death, sadness, laughter, and the like.

Thus, the Sages of the previous ages declared: "In the world to come, there is neither eating, drinking, nor sexual relations. Rather, the righteous will sit with their crowns on their heads and delight in the radiance of the Divine Presence."

From that statement, it is clear that there is no body, for there is no eating or drinking. [Consequently,] the statement, "the righteous sit," must be interpreted metaphorically, i.e., the righteous exist there without work or labor.

Similarly, the phrase, "their crowns on their heads," [is also a metaphor, implying] that they will possess the knowledge that they grasped which allowed them to merit the life of the world to come. This will be their crown. A similar [usage of this metaphor was employed by] Solomon [Song of Songs 3:11]: "The crown with which his mother crowned him."

[Support for the concept that this does not refer to a physical crown can be brought from the prophecy, Isaiah 51:11]: "Eternal joy will be upon their heads." Joy is not a physical entity which can rest on a head. Similarly, the expression "crown" used by the Sages [refers to a spiritual concept], knowledge.

What is meant by the expression, "delight in the radiance of the Divine Presence"? That they will comprehend the truth of G-dliness which they cannot grasp while in a dark and humble body.

3 The term "soul" when used in this context does not refer to the soul which needs the body, but rather to "the form of the soul," the knowledge which it comprehends according to its power. Similarly, it comprehends abstract concepts and other matters. This is "the form" whose nature we described in the fourth chapter of Hilchot Yesodei HaTorah. This is the soul referred to in this context.

Since this life is not accompanied by death - for death is an event associated with the body alone and, in that realm, there is no body - it is called "the bond of life," as [I Samuel 25:29] states: "And the soul of my master will be bound up in the bond of life." This is the reward above which there is no higher reward and the good beyond which there can be [other] good. This was [the good] desired by all the prophets.

4 How many metaphoric terms have been used to refer to [the world to come]! "The mountain of G-d" [Psalms 24:3], "His holy place" [ibid.], "the holy path" [Isaiah 35:8], "the courtyards of G-d" [Psalms 65:5, 92:14], "the pleasantness of G-d" [ibid. 27:4], "the tent of G-d" [ibid. 15:1], "the palace of G-d" [ibid. 5:8], "the house of G-d" [ibid. 27:4], "the gate of G-d" [ibid. 118:20].

The Sages referred to this good which is prepared for the righteous with the metaphor: "the feast." Generally, it is referred to with the term "the world to come."

5 The retribution beyond which there is no greater retribution is that the soul will be cut off and not merit this life as [Numbers 15:31] states: "This soul shall surely be cut off. His sin shall remain upon him."

This refers to the obliteration of the soul which was referred to by the prophets with the following metaphoric terms: "the pit of destruction" [Psalms 55:24], "obliteration" [ibid. 88:12], "the bonfire" [Isaiah 30:33], "the leech" [Proverbs 30:15]. All the synonyms for nullification and destruction are used to refer to it for it is the [ultimate] nullification after which there is no renewal and the [ultimate] loss which can never be recovered.

6 Lest you think lightly of this good, [the world to come], imagining that the reward for the mitzvot and for a person [following] completely the paths of truth is for him to eat and drink good foods, have intercourse with beautiful forms, wear garments of linen and lace, dwell in ivory palaces, use utensils of gold and silver, or other similar ideas, as conceived by the foolish, decadent Arabs, who are flooded with lewdness.

In contrast, the sages and men of knowledge know that all these matters are vain and empty things, without any purpose. They are only considered of great benefit to us in this world because we possess a body and a physical form. All these matters are the needs of the body. The soul only desires them and lusts for them because of the needs of the body, so that its desires will be fulfilled and its health maintained. In a situation, where there is no body, all of these matters will be nullified.

There is no way in this world to grasp and comprehend the ultimate good which the soul will experience in the world to come.

We only know bodily good and that is what we desire. However, that [ultimate] good is overwhelmingly great and cannot be compared to the good of this world except in a metaphoric sense.

In truth, there is no way to compare the good of the soul in the world to come to the bodily goods of this world. Rather, that good is infinitely great, with no comparison or likeness. This is alluded to by David's statement [Psalms 31:20]: "How great is the good that You have hidden for those who fear You."

7 How very much did David desire the life of the world to come as implied by [Psalms 27:13]: "Had I not believed that I would see the goodness of G-d in the land of the living!"

The Sages of the previous generations have already informed us that man does not have the potential to appreciate the good of the world to come in a full sense nor can anyone know its greatness, beauty, and power except G-d, alone.

All the beneficence which the prophets promised Israel in their visions are only physical concerns which Israel will appreciate in the Messianic age when dominion [over the world] will return to Israel. However, the good of the life of the world to come has no comparison or likeness, nor was it described by the prophets, lest with such a description, they diminish it.

This [was implied] by [Isaiah's (64:3)] statement: "No eye has ever seen, 0 G-d, except for You, what You will do for those who wait for You;" i.e. the good which was not perceived by the vision of a prophet and is perceived by G-d alone, this was created by G-d for those who wait for Him.

The Sages declared: "All the prophets only prophesied about the Messianic Age. However, regarding the world to come - `No eye has ever seen, 0 G-d, except for You.'

8 The Sages did not use the expression "the world to come" with the intention of implying that [this realm] does not exist at present or that the present realm will be destroyed and then, that realm will come into being.

The matter is not so. Rather, [the world to come] exists and is present as implied by [Psalms 31:20: "How great is the good] that You have hidden... which You have made...." It is only called the world to come because that life comes to a man after life in this world in which we exist, as souls [enclothed] in bodies. This [realm of existence] is presented to all men at first.

Rabbi Saadia Gaon: If I had known about G-d

Rabbi Saadia Gaon (882-942CE), born in Egypt, was one of the last *Gaonim* and had many hundreds of students.

One morning, two of his students heard a strange sound coming from the other side of a hill. They climbed the hill and looked down to see their master sitting in the snow, weeping, praying, and engaging in other acts of penitence.

This was shocking to them. What could a *tsaddik* (completely righteous person) such as Rabbi Saadia possibly need to repent for?

They hurried away, but as the day progressed they couldn't resist the urge to ask their teacher about what they witnessed.

"I do that every day," he said to them. "Every day I repent and plead with G-d to forgive my shortcomings and failings in my service of Him."

"Your failings?" they asked. "Of what failings does the Gaon speak?"

"Let me tell you a story," said Rabbi Saadiah. "Something that happened to me a while ago."

"At one point in my life, I decided that all the honor and attention I was receiving from everyone around me was interfering with my service of the Creator. G-d must be served with joy, and without complete humility, joy is impossible. So I decided that I would spend several months in a place where no one recognized me.

"I dressed in simple garments and began my self-imposed exile, wandering from town to town. One night I was in a small inn run by an old Jew. He was a very kind and simple man, and we spoke for a while before I went to sleep. Early the next morning, after I had prayed *shacharit* (the morning prayer), I bade him farewell and was again on my way.

"What I didn't know was that several of my pupils had been searching for me, and several hours after I left the inn they appeared, hot on my trail. 'Did you see Rabbi Saadiah Gaon?' they asked him. 'We have reason to believe that he was here.'

"'Saadiah Gaon?' replied the bewildered old Jew. 'What would the great RavSaadiah be doing in a place like mine? Rav Saadiah Gaon in my inn? No . . . I'm sure that you are very mistaken! There was no Rav Saadiah Gaon here!'

"But when the young men described me to him and explained about my exile and 'disguise,' the old Jew grabbed his head and cried: '*Oy!* Rav Saadiah! Rav Saadiah was here! You are right! *Oy, Oy!*' and he ran outside, jumped into his wagon and began urging his horse to go as fast as possible in the direction I had taken.

"After a short time he caught up to me, jumped from his carriage and fell at my feet, weeping: 'Please forgive me, Rav Saadiah. Please forgive me. I didn't know that it was you!'

"I made him stand up and brush himself off, and then said to him: 'But my dear friend, you treated me very well, you were very kind and hospitable. Why are you so sorry? You have nothing to apologize for.'

"'No, no, Rabbi,' he replied. 'If I would have known who you are, I would have served you *completely* differently!'

"Suddenly I realized that this man was teaching me a very important lesson in the service of G-d, and that the purpose of my exile had been fulfilled. I thanked and blessed him, and returned home.

"Since then, every evening when I say the prayer before sleeping, I go over in my mind how I served G-d that day. Then I think of that old innkeeper, and say to myself: '*Oy!* If I had known about G-d in the beginning of the day what I know now, I would have served Him completely differently!'

"And that is what I was repenting for this morning."

TRUE or FALSE

1. It is a positive commandment to confess all of one's sins verbally to G-d and promise never to repeat the act again.

2. Some sins require the death of the person as atonement.

3. Willful sins require a guilt offering and confession to G-d for atonement.

4. If a man injures a colleague or damages his property he must also pay him restitution.

5. All sins, severe and lighter, intentional and inadvertent, are atoned for by the goat sent to Azazel on Yom Kippur, but only if one repents.

6. Severe sins are those of which one is liable for death or to be *karet,* "cut off."

7. Without the Temple and the alter of atonement, no offerings are required, only *teshuvah* "to repent."

8. One reaches complete teshuvah when he is confronted by the same situation and abstains.

9. If a man repents on the last day of his life, all his sins are forgiven.

10. One's teshuvah is not complete until he resolves in his heart to abandon his sin.

11. If one commits a sin against his colleague, it is very praiseworthy for him after he repents to confess his sins publically to make them known to others.

12. If one commits a sin against G-d, it is arrogant to publicize one's transgressions.

13. The essence of the customary confessional prayer is, "For we have all sinned."

14. Teshuvah and Yom Kippur only atone for sins between man and G-d.

15. One must pay restitution to his colleague, appease him, and continually ask for forgiveness until he is forgiven.

16. If a colleague refuses to forgive, he should bring a group of three friends with him three more times, and then may cease pursuing the matter.

17. One who refuses to forgive another is considered as the sinner.

18. One whose merits exceed his sins is righteous, and one whose sins exceed his merits is wicked and will immediately die.

19. The earth was immediately destroyed by the flood because the collective sins of the entire world exceeded the merits.

20. G-d only counts a person's sins against his merits if he committed it three times or more.

21. Every person who does *teshuvah* will be accepted in the world to come.

22. All people have free will to turn himself to the path of good or the path of evil.

23. One who comes to purify himself is helped.

24. One should always count himself as leaning towards death and confess his sins immediately.

25. One must confess also his negative character traits such as anger, hatred, envy, frivolity, pursuit of money and honor, pursuit of gluttony, and the like.

26. One who completes *teshuvah* goes from being hated by G-d, disgusting, far removed, and abominable, to being beloved, desirable, close and dear to G-d.

27. One who repents is more exalted than the one who never sinned at all.

28. It is an utter sin to remind one who has repented of his previous deeds to embarrass him, or even bring up surrounding circumstances or other similar matters so he will recall what he did.

29. Olam Habah is endlessly long, and life will not be accompanied by death, nor good with evil.

30. The wicked will not merit Olam Habah; rather they will be cut off and die and their souls obliterated.

31. In Olam Habah there are no bodies or physical form, or any of the functions associated with bodily functions, only souls of the righteous alone.

32. The righteous souls in Olam Habah will delight in the radiance of the Divine Presence, remembering eternally in joy the knowledge of their good merits.

33. G-d alone possesses the potential to appreciate the full sense of good, greatness, beauty, and power of Olam Habah.

34. Olam Habah exists and is present, but that life only comes to a man after life in this world.

ANSWERS

All answers are TRUE.

WHERE DO
I START?

IF YOU'VE MADE IT THIS FAR, you've already started. Congratulations!

Love HaShem!

(Mishnah Torah, Teshuvah 10)

1 A person should not say: "I will fulfill the mitzvot of the Torah and occupy myself in its wisdom in order to receive all the blessings which are contained within it or in order to merit the life of the world to come."

"[Similarly,] I will separate myself from all the sins which the Torah warned against so that I will be saved from all the curses contained in the Torah or so that [my soul] will not be cut off from the life of the world to come."

It is not fitting to serve G-d in this manner. A person whose service is motivated by these factors is considered one who serves out of fear. He is not on the level of the prophets or of the wise.

The only ones who serve G-d in this manner are common people, women, and minors. They are trained to serve G-d out of fear until their knowledge increases and they serve out of love.

2 One who serves [G-d] out of love occupies himself in the Torah and the mitzvot and walks in the paths of wisdom for no ulterior motive: not because of fear that evil will occur, nor in order to acquire benefit. Rather, he does what is true because it is true, and ultimately, good will come because of it.

This is a very high level which is not merited by every wise man. It is the level of our Patriarch, Abraham, whom G-d described as, "he who loved Me," for his service was only motivated by love.

G-d commanded us [to seek] this rung [of service] as conveyed by Moses as [Deuteronomy 6:5] states: "Love G-d, your L-rd." When a man will love G-d in the proper manner, he will immediately perform all of the mitzvot motivated by love.

3 What is the proper [degree] of love? That a person should love G-d with a very great and exceeding love until his soul is bound up in the love of G-d. Thus, he will always be obsessed with this love as if he is lovesick.

[A lovesick person's] thoughts are never diverted from the love of that woman. He is always obsessed with her; when he sits down, when he gets up, when he eats and drinks. With an even greater [love], the love for G-d should be [implanted] in the hearts of those who love Him and are obsessed with Him at all times as we are commanded [Deuteronomy 6:5: "Love G-d...] with all your heart and with all your soul."

This concept was implied by Solomon [Song of Songs 2:5] when he stated, as a metaphor: "I am lovesick." [Indeed,] the totality of the Song of Songs is a parable describing [this love].

4 The Sages of the previous generations declared: Should one say: "I will study Torah in order that I become wealthy, in order that I be called a Rabbi, or in' order that I receive reward in the world to come?" The Torah teaches [Deuteronomy 11:13]: "[If you are careful to observe My commandments...]" to love G-d; [implying] that all that you do should only be done out of love.

The Sages also said: [Psalms 112:1] "Desire His commandments greatly." [Desire His commandments] and not the reward [which comes from] His commandments.

In a similar manner, the great Sages would command the more understanding and brilliant among their students in private: "Do not be like servants who serve their master [for the sake of receiving a reward].' Rather, since He is the Master, it is fitting to serve Him;" i.e., serve [Him] out of love.

5 Anyone who occupies himself with the Torah in order to receive reward or in order to protect himself from retribution is considered as one who is not occupied for the G-d's sake.

[In contrast,] anyone who occupies himself with it, not because of fear, nor to receive a reward, but rather because of his love for the L-rd of the entire earth who commanded it, is one who occupies himself for G-d's sake.

Nevertheless, our Sages declared: A person should always occupy himself with the Torah even when it is not for G-d's sake for out of [service which is not intended] for G-d's sake will come service that is intended for G-d's sake.

Therefore, when one teaches children, women, and most of the common people, one should teach them to serve out of fear and in order to receive a reward. As their knowledge grows and their wisdom increases, this secret should be revealed to them [slowly,] bit by bit. They should become accustomed to this concept gradually until they grasp it and know it and begin serving [G-d] out of love.

6 It is a well-known and clear matter that the love of G-d will not become attached within a person's heart until he becomes obsessed with it at all times as is fitting, leaving all things in the world except for this. This was implied by the command [Deuteronomy 6:5: "Love G-d, your L-rd,] with all your heart and all your soul."

One can only love G-d [as an outgrowth] of the knowledge with which he knows Him. The nature of one's love depends on the nature of one's knowledge! A small [amount of knowledge arouses] a lesser love. A greater amount of knowledge arouses a greater love.

Therefore, it is necessary for a person to seclude himself in order to understand and conceive wisdom and concepts which make his creator known to him according to the potential which man possesses to understand and comprehend as we explained in Hilchot Yesodei HaTorah.

Rabbi Shimon: For the Sake of the Mitzvah

Rabbi Shimon Bar Yochai lived in the 2nd century CE in Israel and was one of the great *Tannaim*, son-in-law to the wondrous

Rabbi Pinchas ben Yair. Rabbi Shimon was the pupil of Rabbi Akiva, and never left his teacher's side until Rabbi Akiva died a martyr's death for teaching Torah publically.

Rabbi Akiva spent his final moments on earth reciting the Shema, accepting upon himself the yoke of Heaven. His students asked him: "Our teacher, this far?!" He answered:

The Shema teaches us to love God with all our souls (Deuteronomy 6:5), which I understood to mean "even if they are taking your soul." My entire life I agonized over this verse: Would I really love God even if my soul were being taken? I at last have the opportunity to demonstrate this. How could I not do so now?

And as the rabbi recited "HaShem is one" his soul left him.

Rabbi Shimon later became the head of the Sanhedrin after hiding in a cave for 13 years with his son, Rabbi Elazar, fleeing from Roman persecution for teaching Torah. He was possibly the holiest man that ever lived. He authored the *Zohar*, was a master of the Oral Torah, and was well known as a miracle worker. He was one of the few Jews in history who spent every instant of his time learning Torah; no casual conversations or breaks.

Everyone was surprised when the day after Rosh Hashanah he showed up at the door of his nephews' home and began to lecture them about the importance of giving charity to the poor.

Although they didn't really have money to spare and totally didn't understand the urgency of what he was saying, they listened attentively.

When Rabbi Shimon spoke everyone listened.

"Give with an open hand," Rabbi Shimon adjured. "Don't worry about tomorrow, G-d will provide. And most important: write it all down. Every penny you give, write it down and carry the list with you at all times. I want to see a big sum at the end of the year."

Rabbi Shimon made them promise, and he left.

Almost a year later they had another strange visit from a posse of Roman soldiers with an order for their arrest. Someone accused them of selling silk without paying the tax to the government. They began weeping and protesting their innocence but to no avail.

Trembling with fear, they were led off to prison where they were given a choice: either pay an outrageous fine of six hundred dinar or produce an even more outrageously priced silk garment for the king, both of which were utterly beyond their means.

When Rabbi Shimon heard what had happened he immediately rushed to the prison and got special permission to visit his relatives.

"Where is the account of the charity you gave?" He asked. "How much did you give?"

"Here," they replied as one of them pulled the small parchment from his pocket.

Rabbi Shimon took the account and noticed that they had given almost six hundred dinar; they were just six dinar short. "Do you have any money with you?" he asked.

They produced six dinar that they had sewn into their garments in case they needed it. Rabbi Shimon took the money, bribed one of the officials, the charges were dropped and they were released.

Rabbi Shimon explained to them what had happened. "This past Rosh Hashanah I dozed off and dreamt that the government would demand of you six hundred dinars. That is why I told you to give charity, to negate the decree."

"Then why didn't you tell us about that?" they complained. "We would have given the money immediately and spared ourselves a lot of anguish."

"But then," replied Rabbi Shimon. "You wouldn't have done the mitzvah for its own sake."

Learn from kosher sources

Beware that there are groups under false teachers out there that call themselves Jews and are not. Also, there are some groups that call themselves Noahides yet teach worship of false gods.

To make sure you remain in kosher teaching, verify that the group is under Orthodox Rabbinic supervision. Find out who the Rabbi is, and where he received his Rabbinic title from. If the leader is not an Orthodox Rabbi or under the supervision of an Orthodox rabbi, it's best to stay away from that group and their teachings until they have proper oversight.

Netiv.net is a rich pool of kosher resources, created with you in mind. You can also participate in the live sessions throughout the week. Get connected.

Chumash

One should start by studying the Written Torah and then move on to studying *Torah Shebaal Peh.*

Start with buying a *chumash.* A *chumash* is a book that contains the Written Torah and kosher commentary, much of which comes straight from Rashi. The *chumash* is divided up cleanly into each *parashah* (Torah portion for the week), and each *aliyah* (Torah reading for the day).

The recommended version is the Stone Edition *chumash* which has a blue cover with the Hebrew and English side by side on each page. It can be purchased at Netiv.net.

Read the *parashah* each week along with the commentary on each page. The *chumash* also includes the corresponding *haftora* readings from the *Nevi'im* (Prophets) that are read along with the *parashah* each week.

For more information and learning materials from kosher sources, or if you desire to connect to a Noahide community that's under Orthodox Rabbinic supervision, please visit Netiv.net.

Tenakh

Get a *Tenakh* with Hebrew and English. This will become important as you start to learn Hebrew. The *Tenakh* is the Jewish Bible, and it is a "must have" for anyone on the path of learning. There are several kosher versions of *Tenakh* available for purchase at Netiv.net.

The Seven

Familiarize yourself with the Seven Laws of Noah. Study them, examine your own life, and strip away the things that are in violation of the Noahide Laws. Do *teshuvah*. The section of this book called *NOAHIDE LAWS* was compiled for this purpose. If you have any questions about the Seven, contact us through Netiv.net.

Learning Hebrew

Learning Hebrew is great, but not necessary as a Noahide. There are many online resources for this if you are inclined to learn, but be cautious of teachers with an agenda to slip in their idolatrous beliefs. This is a common tactic, and you should be aware of it.

Should I go to a synagogue?

All Jews should attend synagogue.

Unless you were born from Jewish parents or converted to Judaism under proper rabbinic authority, you are not a Jew. Blood tests are not used in Judaism to determine whether one is a Jew or not.

If you are not recognized by Judaism as a Jew, it is not necessary for you to attend synagogue. As a side note, be mindful not to call yourself a Jew if you're not, as it can be very offensive to the suffering and heritage of real Jews.

As a non-Jew, you should only consider visiting a synagogue if you are keeping the Seven Laws of Noah. If you believe in the Christian Bible and/or any form of religion taught by the "New Testament" do not attempt to attend synagogue. It would be highly disrespectful to the Jewish people and the entire belief system of Judaism. A synagogue is a place of prayer for those who worship exclusively the G-d of Israel as defined by Orthodox Judaism.

If you really want to attend synagogue as a righteous Noahide gentile, call your local Orthodox Rabbi and have an honest discussion with him, and ask if it is appropriate for you to sit in the back quietly and observe as a non-Jew.

There is a dress code, and you need to learn the basic rules of synagogue attendance in order to be respectful of these magnificent people that have been guarding and preserving the Torah for thousands of years.

Ask the rabbi, and respect whatever he tells you.

Conversion

If you are not Jewish, you don't need to be Jewish. Unlike other religions, Judaism does not require people to convert in order to participate meaningfully or be a righteous person, nor does Judaism proselytize.

If you're not already practicing the Seven, this is your starting point before you even begin approaching conversion. If you really want to convert, talk to your local Orthodox Rabbi.

What will my friends and family think?

This can be very intimidating, but don't worry about it. It's very likely that your fear is exaggerated in your mind.

But here's a little tip. When you learn something new from the Torah, let it take root internally and become an integral part of who you are before sharing it with others.

This will save you a world of trouble, especially when interacting with others who don't understand. Just be a simple student, and allow HaShem to transform your life with His Torah.

One of the reasons this text exists is to communicate the basic ideas of Judaism clearly in a way that anybody can understand by simply taking a little time to read this book. If you find it difficult to communicate these ideas, just give them a copy of this book.

If they really want to know, they'll read it. This will at least give you something to discuss, but it also can ease their mind that you're not inventing a new religion or following some new fad. You are joining with Israel to participate in the Creator's universe in the appropriate manner.

The world of Torah is beautiful. Don't be overly concerned about what people think about you, what to call yourself, or where you might end up. Take one little bite of Torah at a time and digest it. It's delicious! You'll be back for more.

The Torah is already changing you, so let the Torah do its work. HaShem will take you where He wants you.

And remember, we're all in this together!

Shalom!

May HaShem bless you and guard you.
May HaShem shine His countenance upon you and be gracious to you.
May HaShem turn His countenance toward you and grant you peace.
(Numbers 6:24-26)

INDEX

1886CE, 53
200CE, 37
353-349BCE, 31
358CE, 24
410-310BCE, 24, 31
422BCE, 31
500CE, 49
613, 65, 66, 67, 68
Adam, 75, 76
adultery, 76, 83, 84
Akedah, 122
Aleph-Beit, 17
aliyah, 18, 159
Ammoraim, 43
Ammoriam, 44
Anshei K'nesset Hagedolah,
    24, 25, 31
Av Beit Din, 33
Babylonian, 24, 43, 44
Bamidbar, 17
Beit Din, 33, 53
Beit HaMikdash, 43
bereishit, 18
Bereishit, 17
Bnei Noach, 68
chumash, 158, 159
convert, 67, 161
courts of justice, 76, 85
cursing G-d, 76, 81
derash, 57
Devarim, 17
diaspora, 24
Even Ha'ezer, 53
false G-ds, 76, 77, 158
Gemarah, 43, 44, 50
Geon, 49

Geonim, 49, 52
Great Sanhedrin, 31, 32
halacha, 53, 70
Hebrew, 17, 18, 159, 160
Hillel, 25, 33, 34
idolatry, 32
Khethuvim, 17
Kodashim, 38
kohen, 66
Kohen HaGadol, 68
Kohen HaMashiach, 111
mashach, 111
mashiach, 109
Melech HaMashiach, 111, 112
Men of the Great Assembly,
    24, 31, 32
mesechtot, 39
Messianic Era, 114
Mishnah, 32, 37, 43, 44
Mishnah Torah, 76
mitzvot, 23, 32, 65, 66, 68
Moed, 38
murder, 76, 82
Nashim, 38
Nasi, 33
Netiv, 158, 159
Nevi'im, 17, 24, 159
Nezikin, 38
Noah, 67, 68, 69, 75, 76, 77,
    159, 160
Noahide, 68, 76, 77, 117, 159,
    160
non-Jew, 5, 66, 67, 68, 69, 70,
    76, 160
olam haba, 68
Orach Chayim, 53

Oral Torah, 23
parashah, 18, 159
parashat hashavua, 17
pardes, 57
Passover, 122, 123
peshat, 57
prophesy, 32, 33
Rabbi Joseph Karo, 52
Rabbinic decree, 32
Rambam, 49, 50, 69
Rashi, 49, 158
Rav Ashi, 24
religion, 58, 60, 69, 70, 76, 77
remez, 57
Rishonim, 49, 52
Romans, 44
Romm publishing house, 53
Sanhedrin, 31, 33
Scripture, 33
sefer, 17
seven, 18, 43, 67, 68, 69, 75,
    76, 77, 85, 159, 160, 161
Shammai, 25, 33, 34
Shemot, 17

Shulchan Aruch, 52
sidarim, 38, 39
sod, 57
Sod, 57
Suggiah, 43
synagogue, 18, 53, 160
Talmud, 5, 43, 44, 49, 52, 53
Tannaim, 34, 43, 44
Tenakh, 17, 32
theft, 76, 84, 85
Thirteen Principles of Jewish
    Faith, 117
Tohoroth, 38
Torah, 17
Torah Shebaal Peh, 23, 24, 37,
    76, 158
Vayikra, 17
Written Torah, 76, 158
yeshiva, 44
yeshivot, 44
Yoreh De'ah, 53
Zekenim, 24
Zeraim, 38
Zuggot, 33, 34, 43